THIS BOOK BELONGS TO:

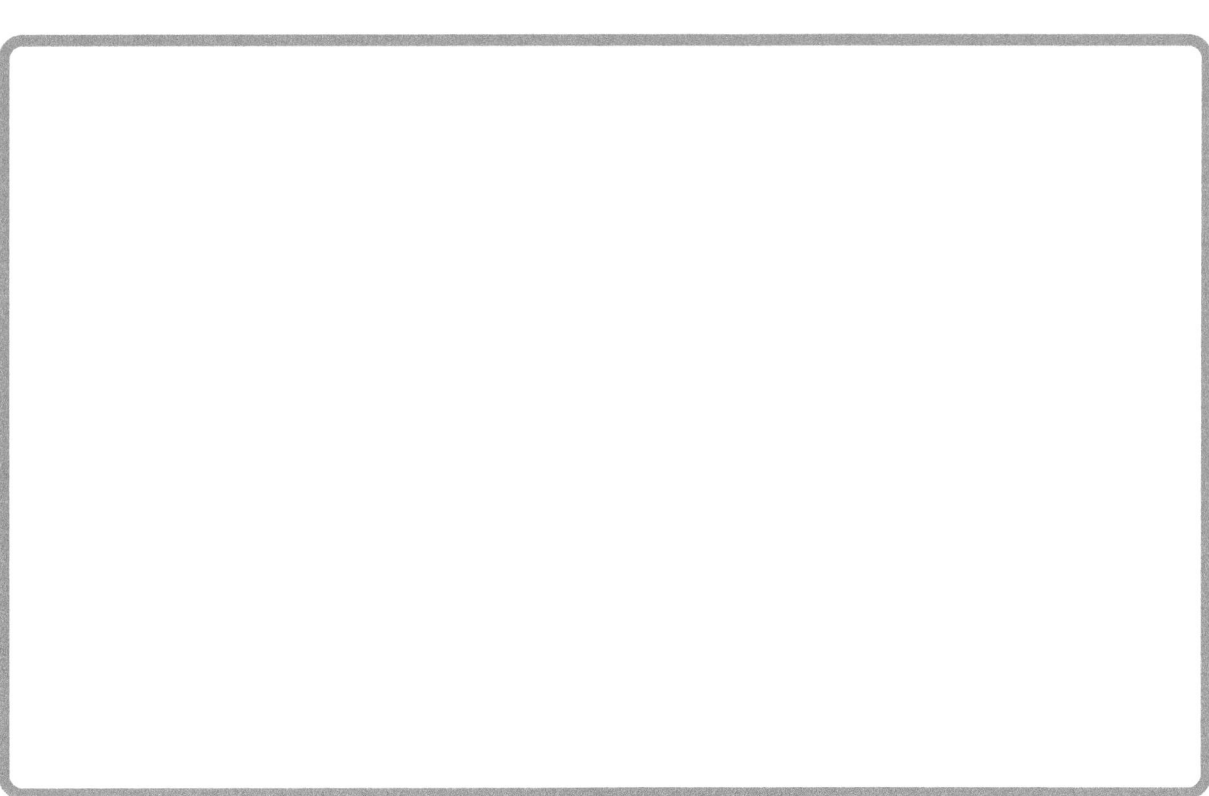

MY FIRST
How to Draw
WORKBOOK FOR KIDS

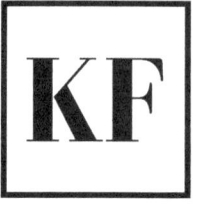

KAY FLEMING

ISBN: 9798705041732 (Paperback)

First printing edition February 2021.

TABLE OF CONTENTS

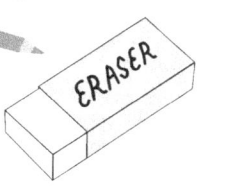

Getting Started

Before you begin, gather all the tools you'll need.

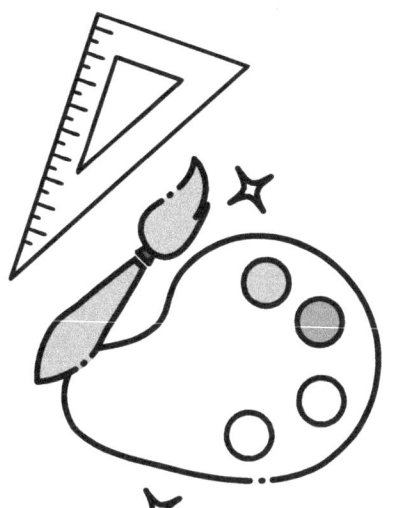

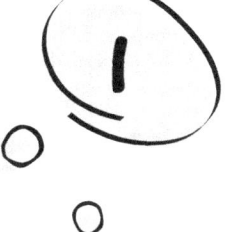

1 Pencil

A fancy pencil is not needed. Choose one that feels good in your hand.

Tip: Always sketch lightly when first starting out. This way, it's easy to erase if you make mistakes.

2 Eraser

A good quality eraser is extremely important to have.

Tip: Avoid using the one at the top of your pencil, if possible.

3 Color

Colored pencils and crayons are good for your finished product.

4 Ruler (Optional)

A ruler comes in handy whenever you need to make straight lines.

Recognizing Shapes

One of the best way to learn how to draw is to practice looking for the shapes that make up objects.

Some shapes are easier to spot than others. It's important to know all your shapes so that you can spot them all while drawing.

Easy to spot

Not so easy to spot:

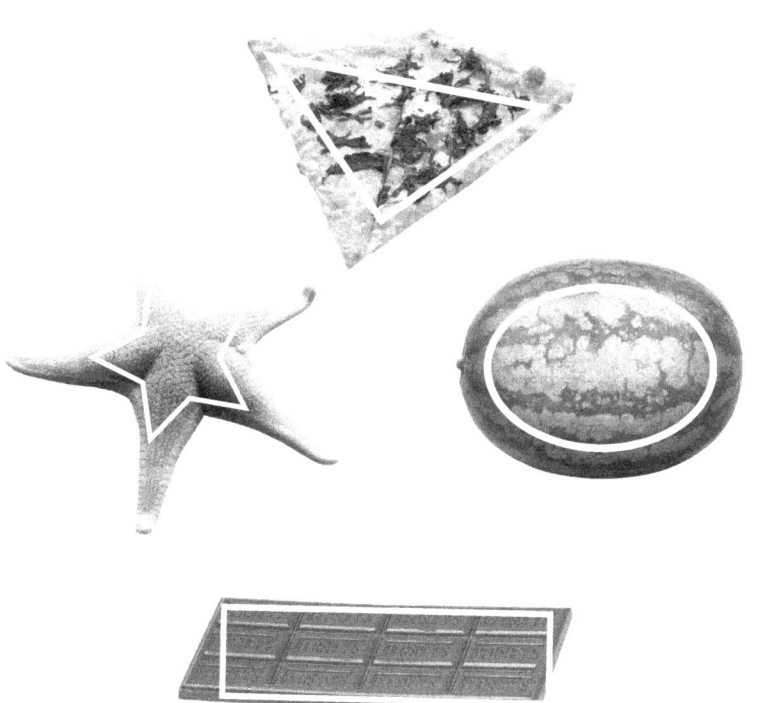

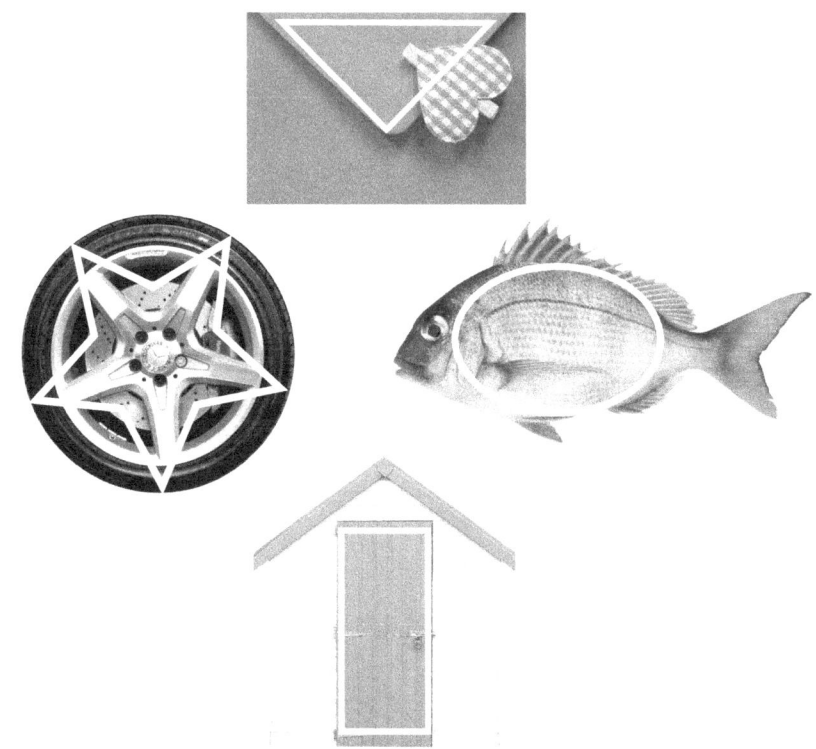

Shapes to know

These are the shapes you want to know. Can you match them to the correct pictures on the right?

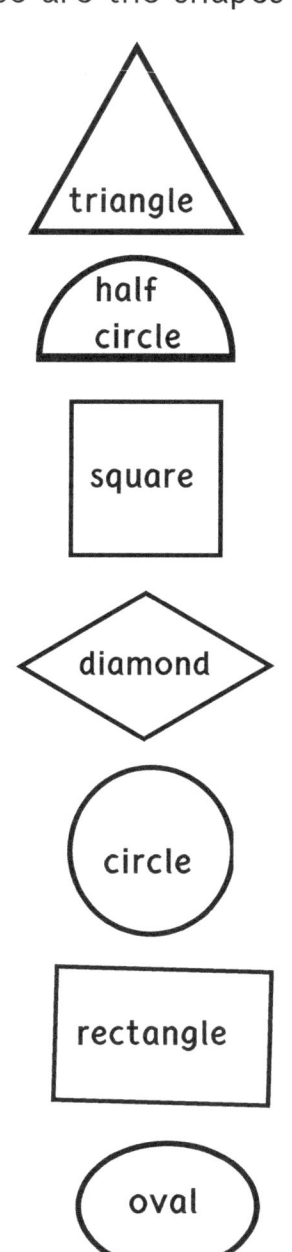

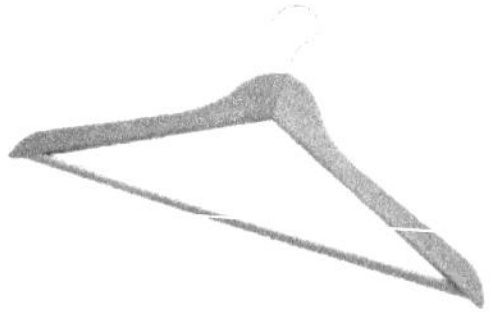

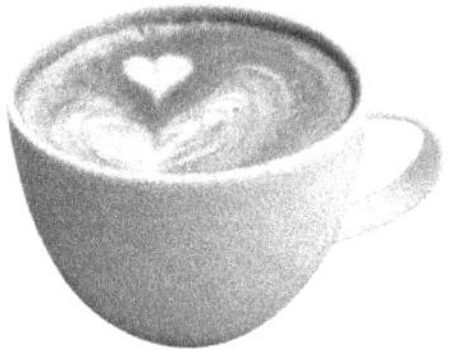

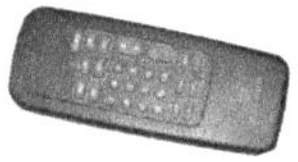

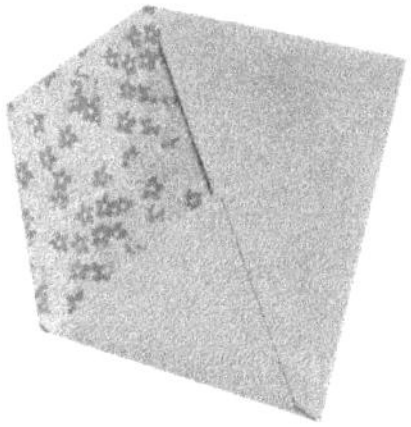

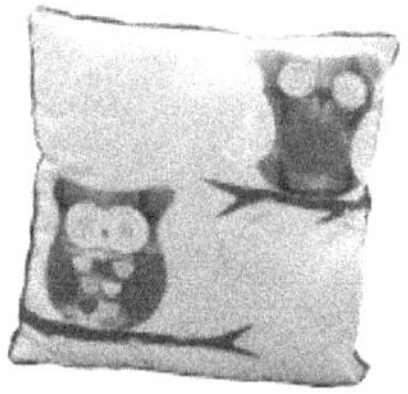

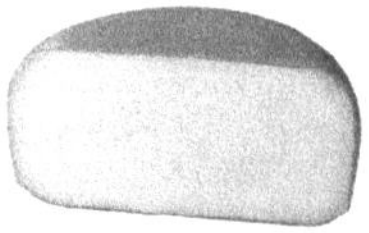

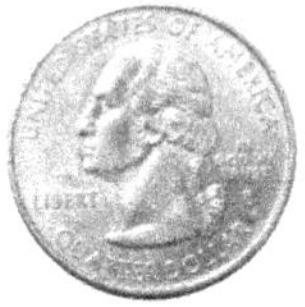

Shape Tracing & Drawing Practice

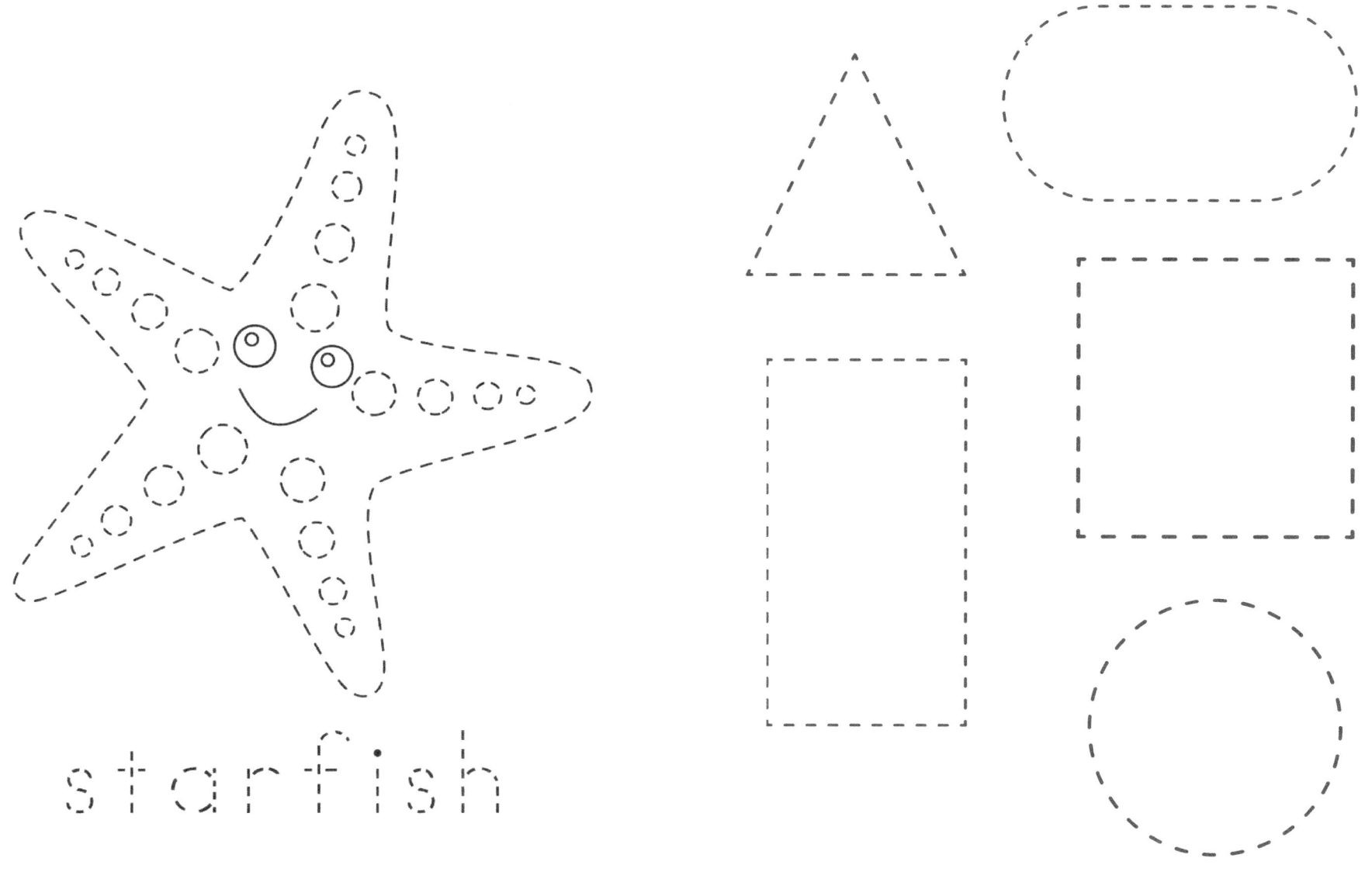

starfish

Learning Lines

Lines are just as important as the shapes we draw. These are the type of lines you need to learn:

Straight

Angle

Spiral

Wavy

Zig zag

Loopy

Curvy

Squiggly

Scallop

TRACE

THEN, DRAW

TRACE

DRAW

TRACE

DRAW

TRACE

DRAW

Line Tracing & Drawing Practice

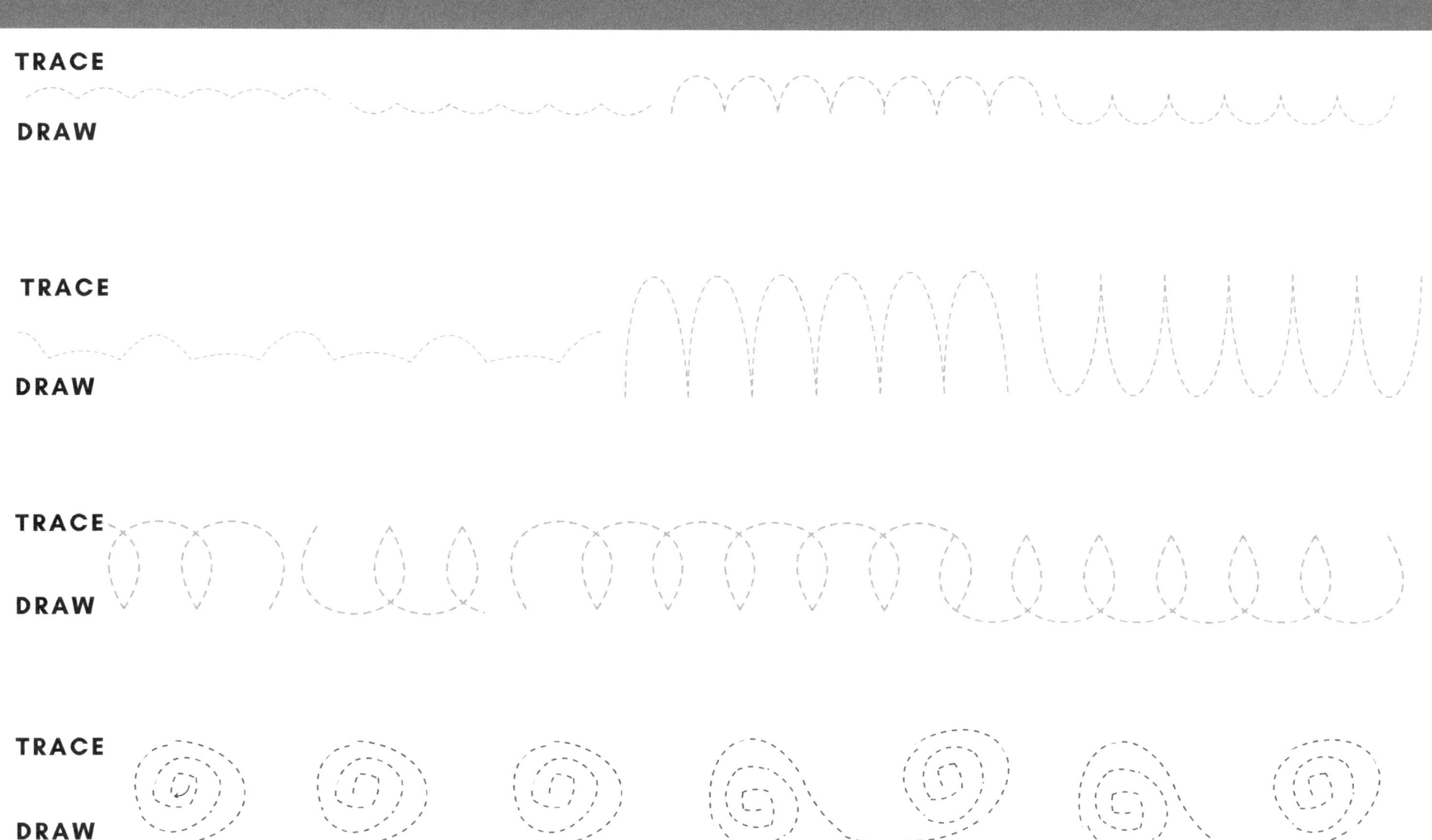

TRACE

DRAW

TRACE

DRAW

TRACE

DRAW

TRACE

DRAW

Picture Tracing & Drawing Practice

Dolphin

Squid

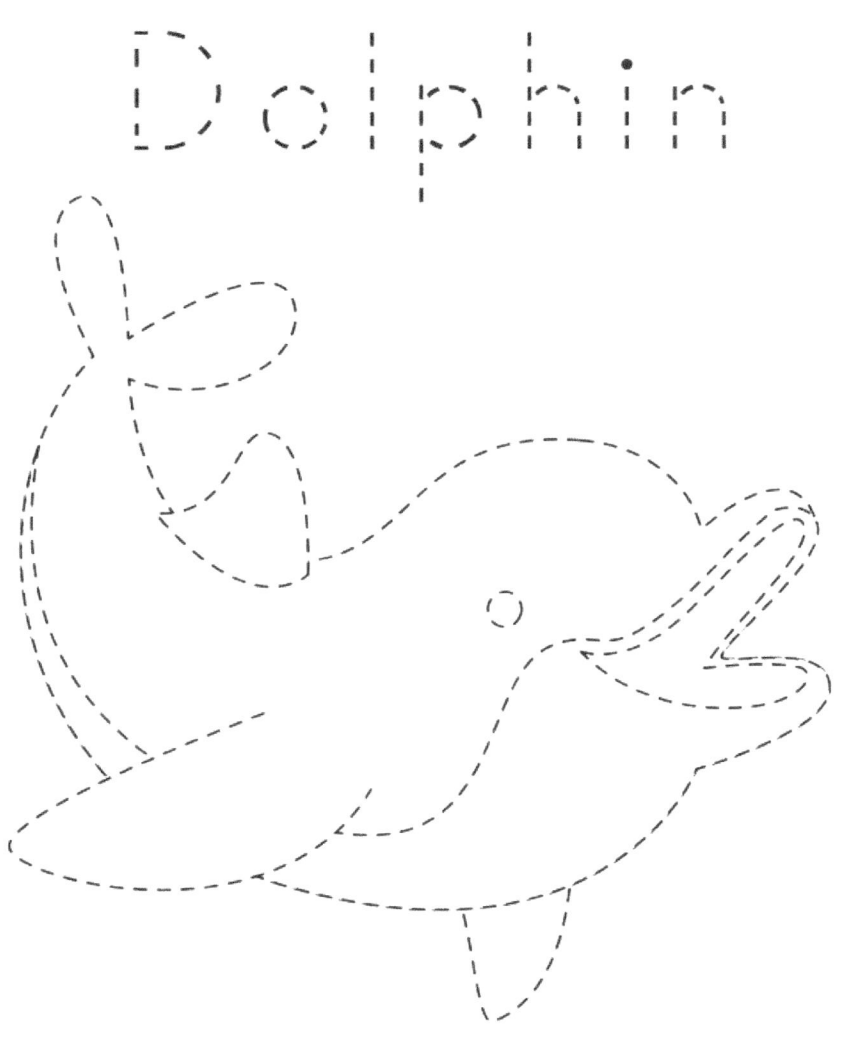

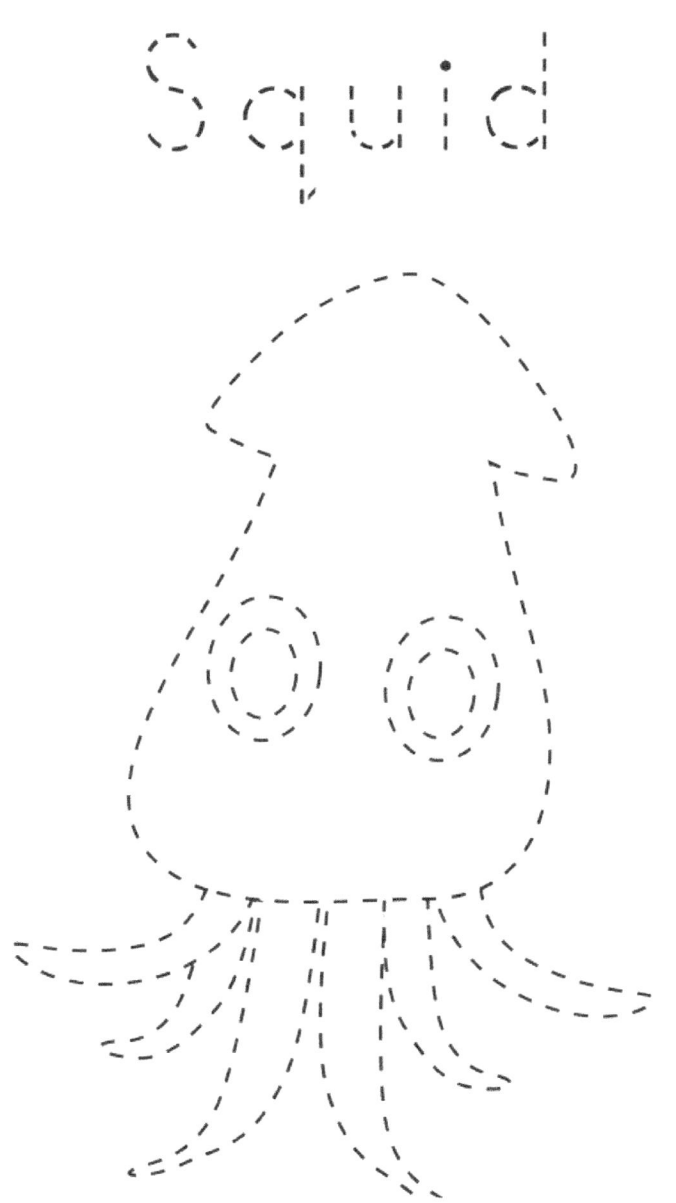

Picture Tracing & Drawing Practice

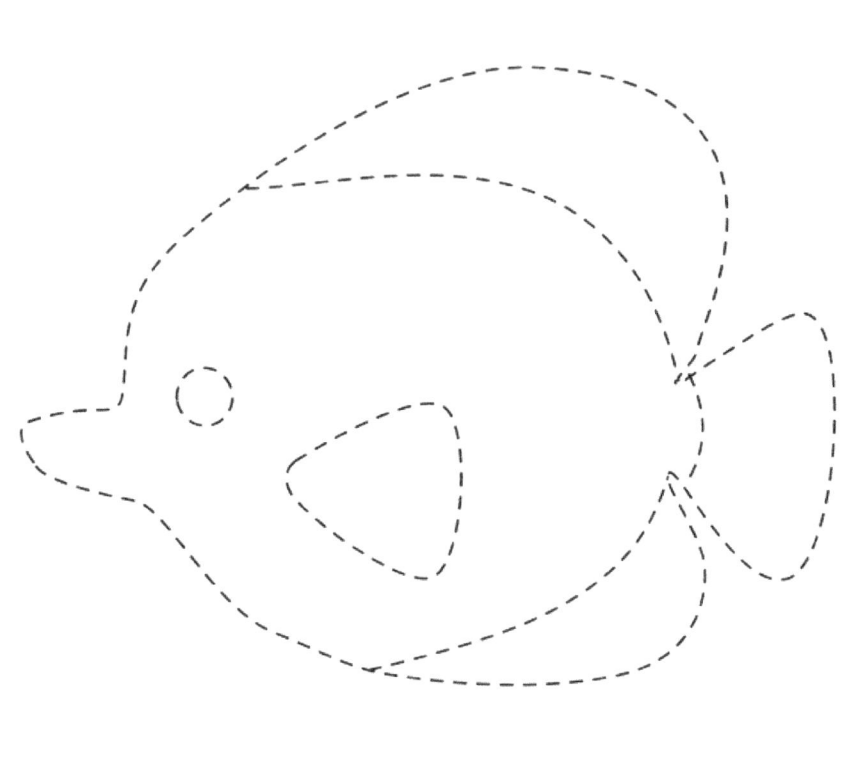

fish

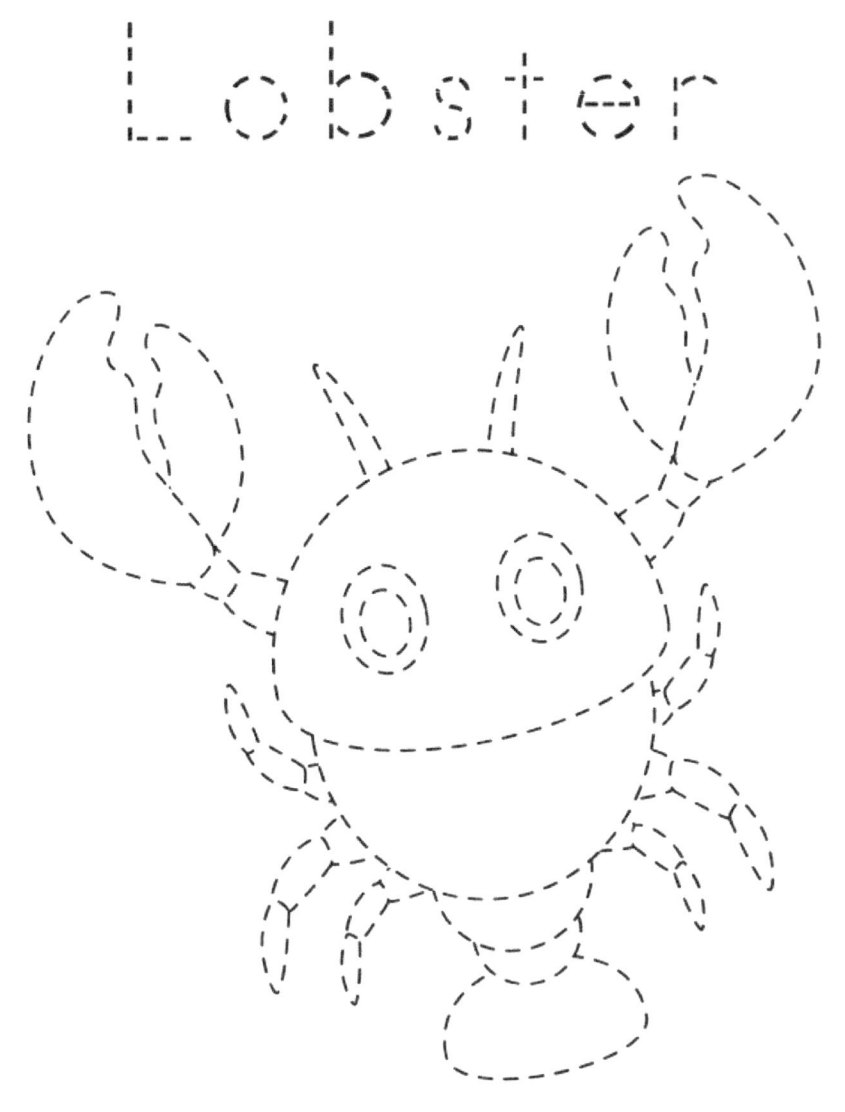

Lobster

Draw each of the steps in order. Then, add details. Color to complete the picture.

Draw Here:

Fish

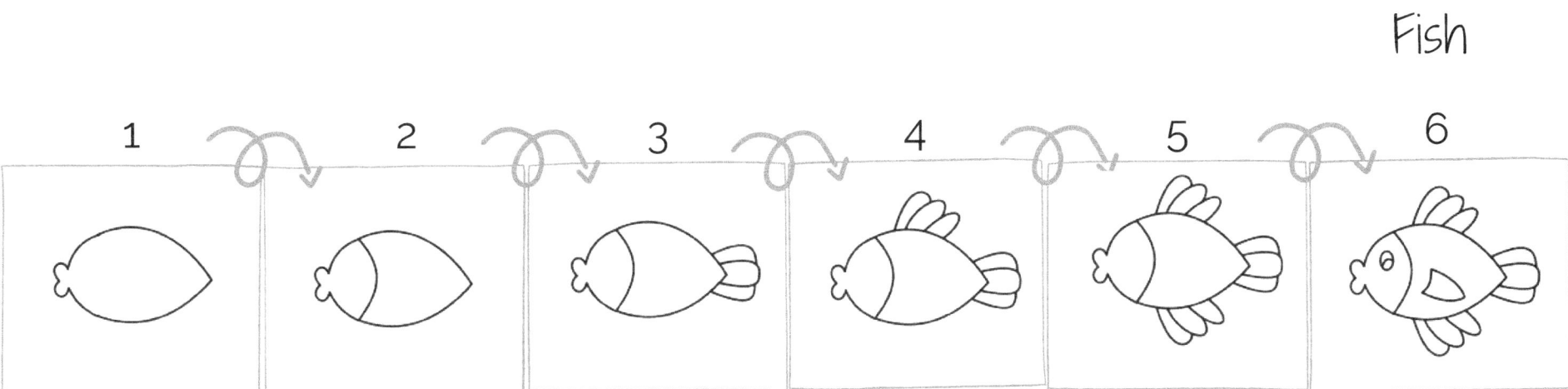

1   2   3   4   5   6

Draw each of the steps in order. Then, add details. Color to complete the picture.

Draw Here:

Fish

1   2   3   4   5   6

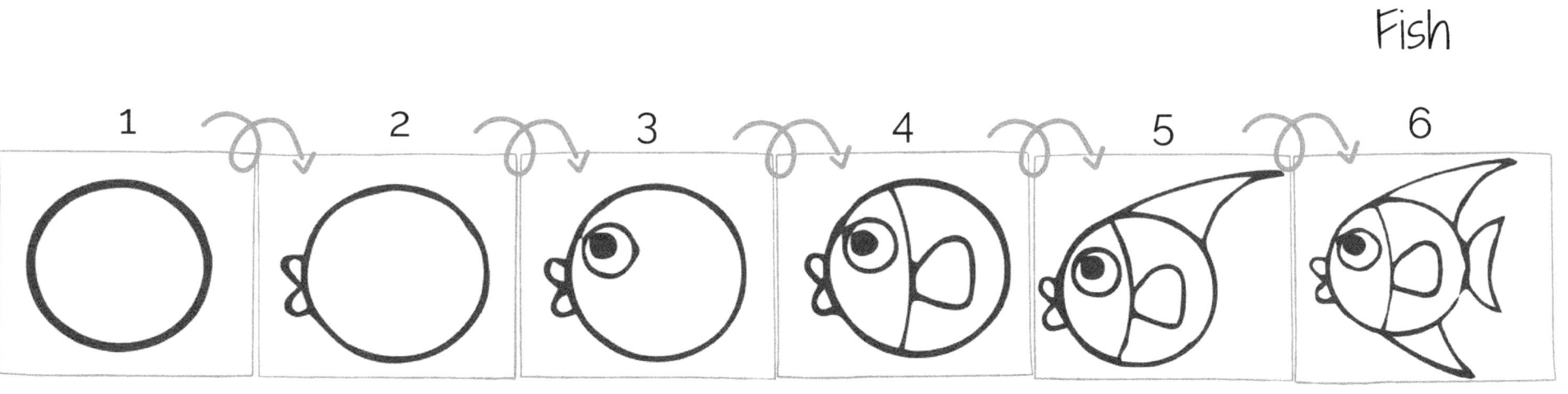

Draw each of the steps in order. Then, add details. Color to complete the picture.

Draw Here:

fish

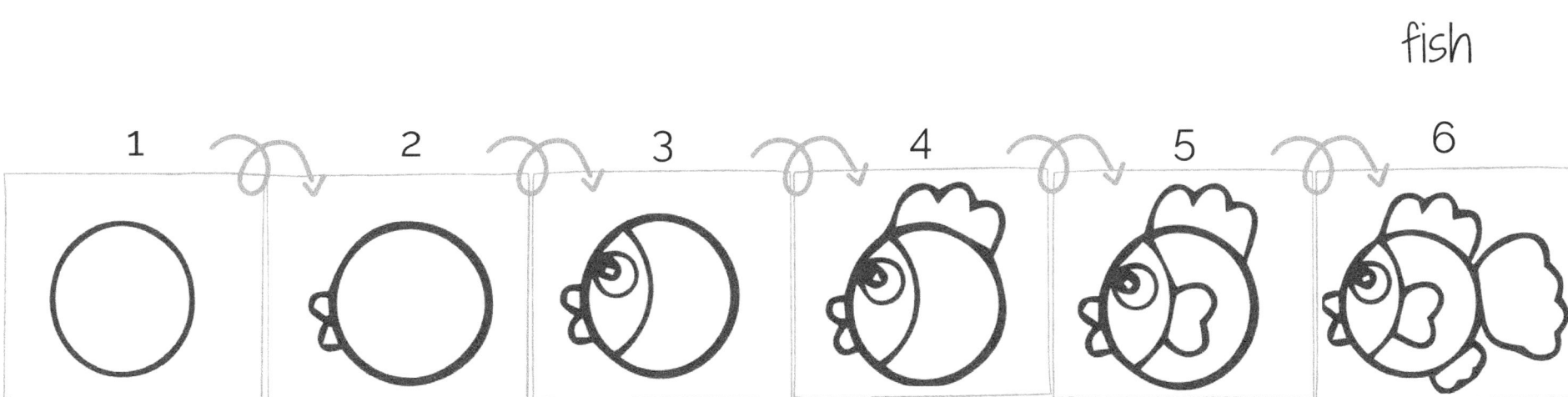

1   2   3   4   5   6

Draw each of the steps in order. Then, add details. Color to complete the picture.

Draw Here:

Crab

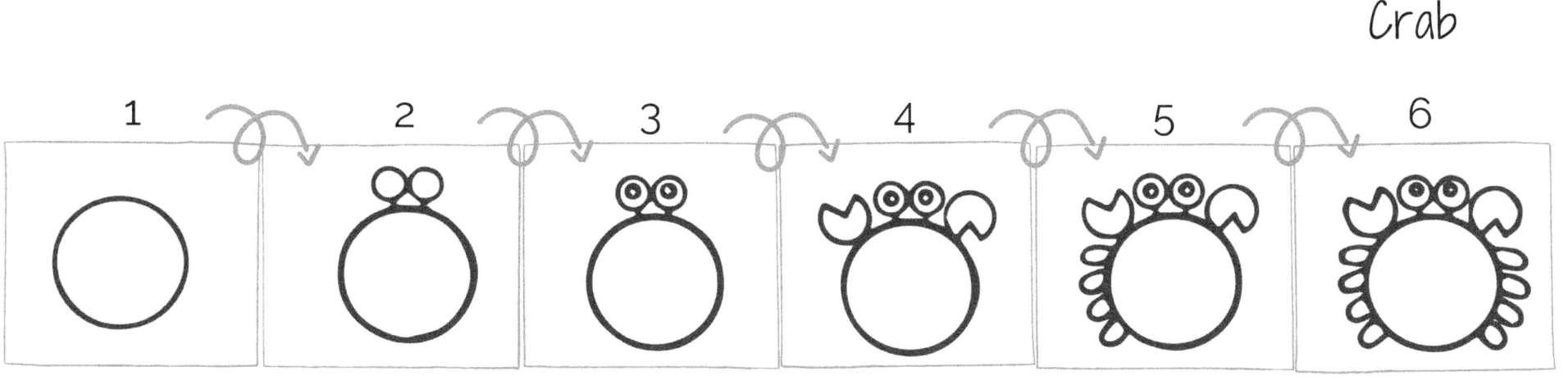

1　　2　　3　　4　　5　　6

Draw each of the steps in order. Then, add details. Color to complete the picture.

Draw Here:

Crab

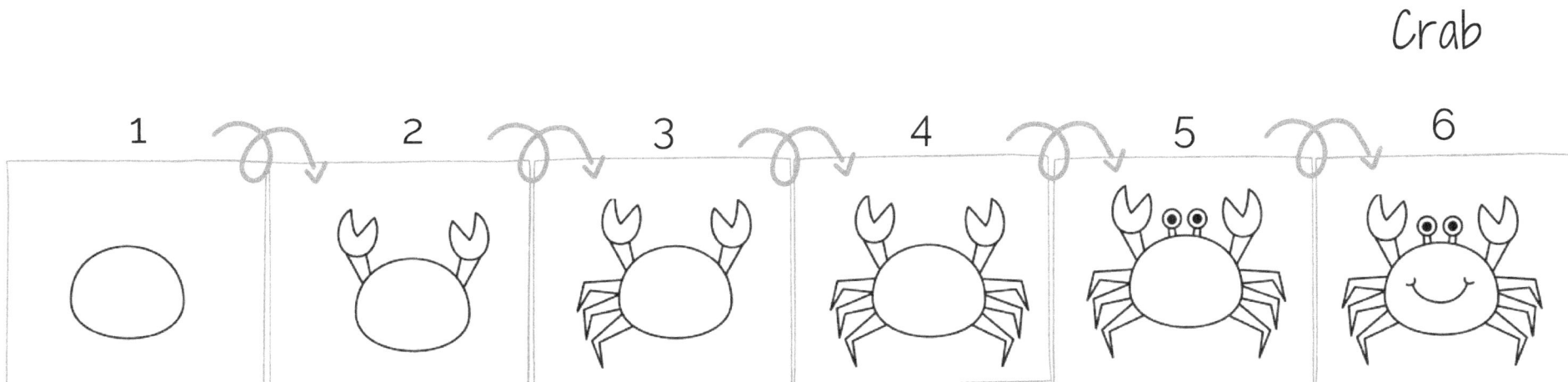

1   2   3   4   5   6

Draw each of the steps in order. Then, add details. Color to complete the picture.

Draw Here:

Snail

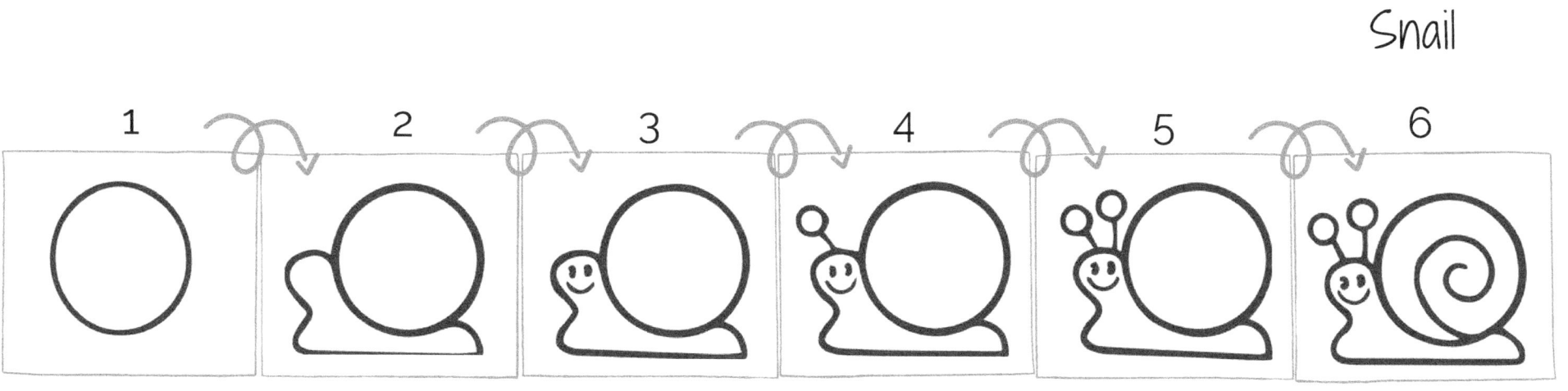

Draw each of the steps in order. Then, add details. Color to complete the picture.

Draw Here:

Snail

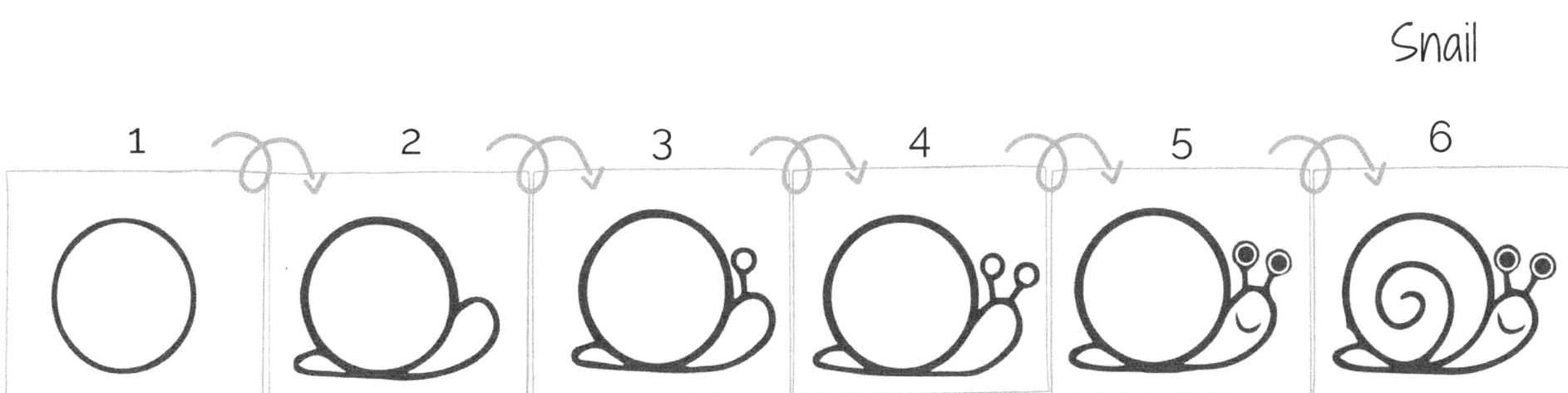

1 2 3 4 5 6

Draw each of the steps in order. Then, add details. Color to complete the picture.

Draw Here:

Turtle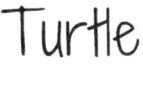

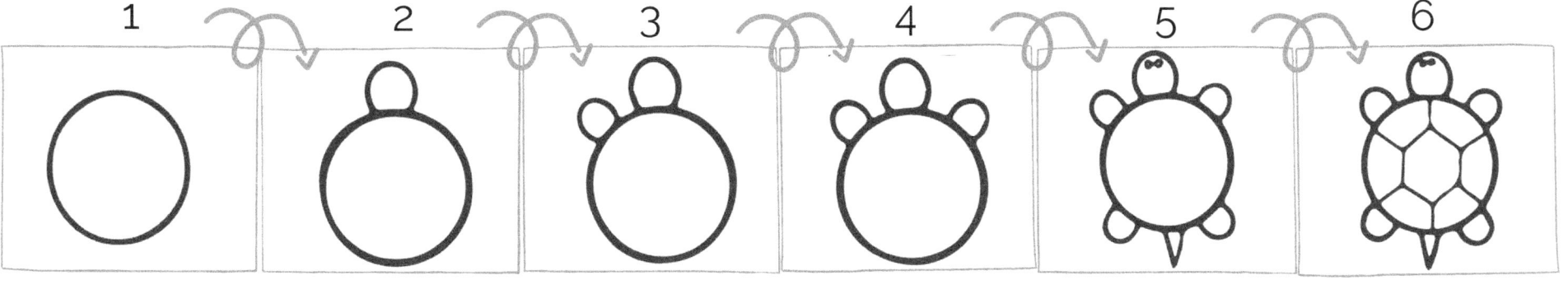

1   2   3   4   5   6

Draw each of the steps in order. Then, add details. Color to complete the picture.

Draw Here:

Turtle

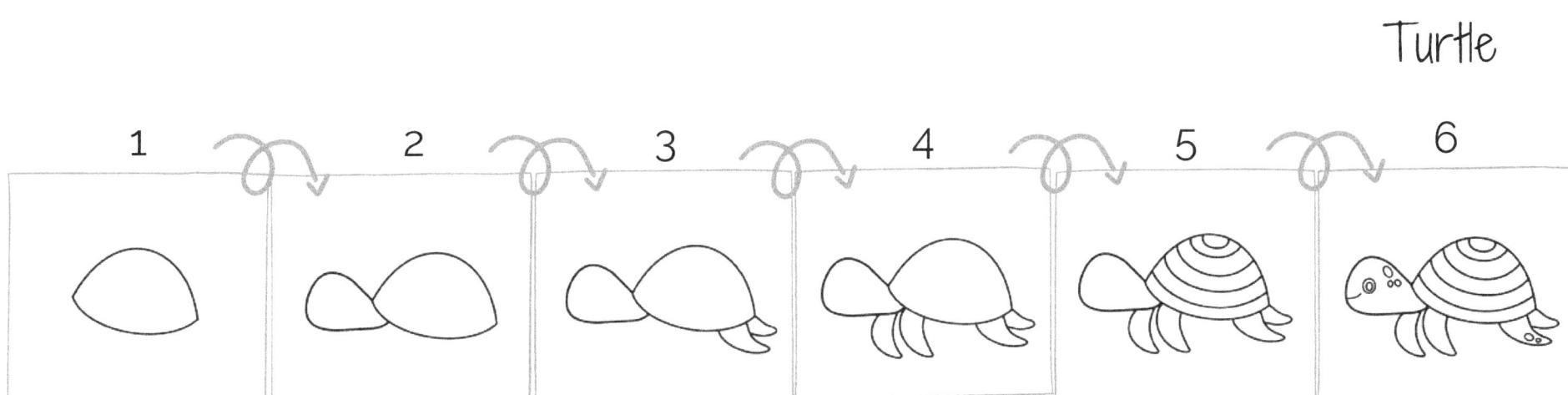

1   2   3   4   5   6

21

Draw each of the steps in order. Then, add details. Color to complete the picture.

Draw Here:

Octopus

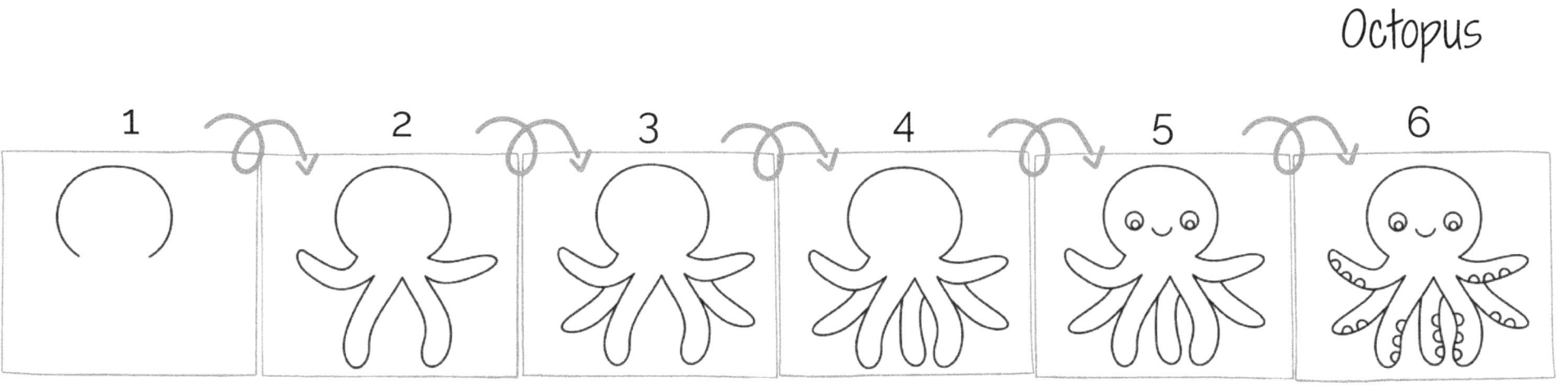

Draw each of the steps in order. Then, add details. Color to complete the picture.

Draw Here:

Shark

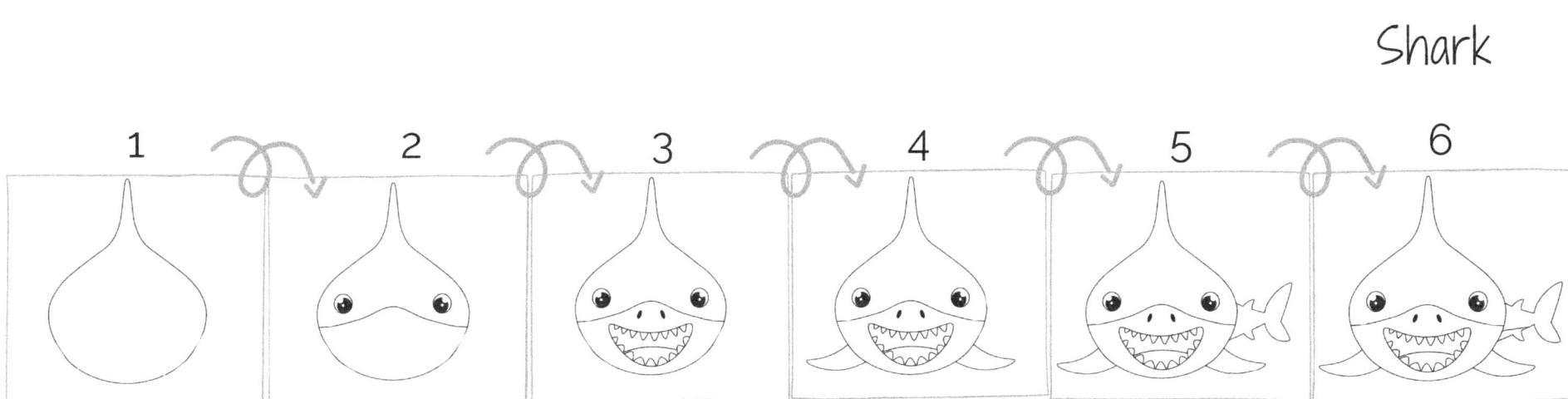

1   2   3   4   5   6

Draw each of the steps in order. Then, add details. Color to complete the picture.

Draw Here:

Palm tree

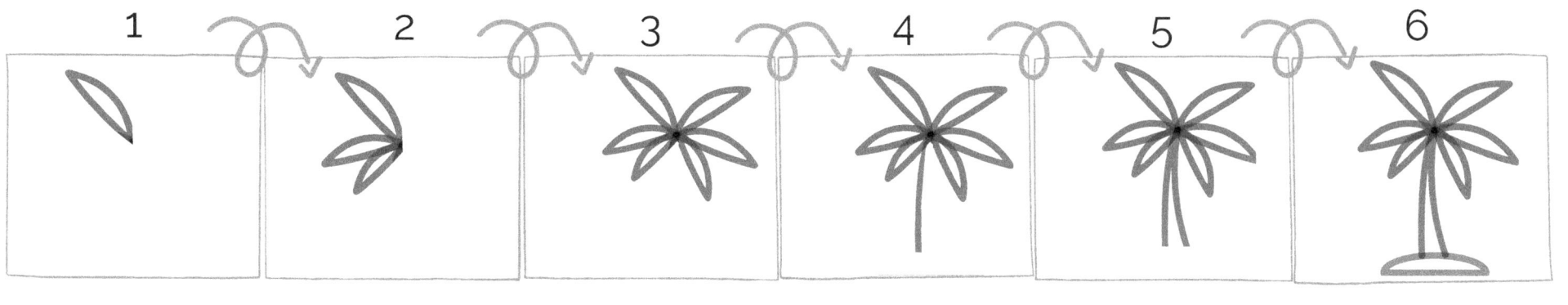

1 2 3 4 5 6

Draw each of the steps in order. Then, add details. Color to complete the picture.

Draw Here:

Ocean scene

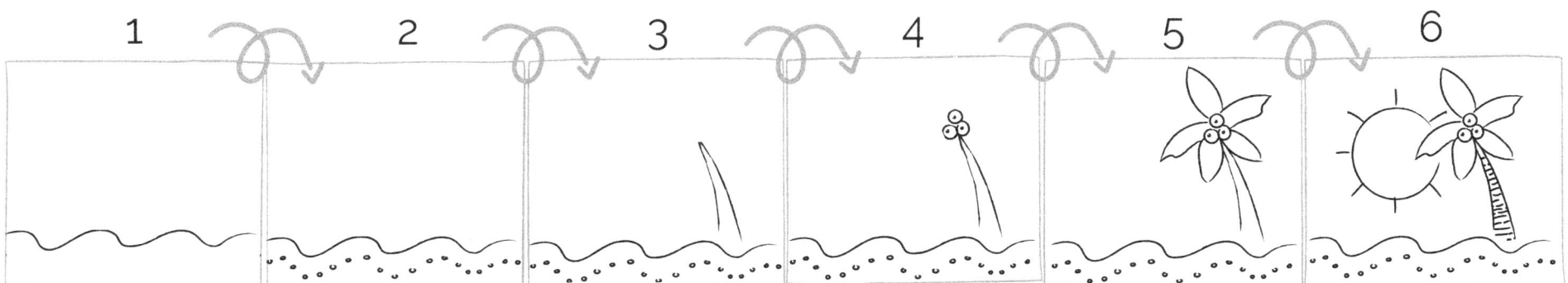

Draw each of the steps in order. Then, add details. Color to complete the picture.

Draw Here:

Submarine

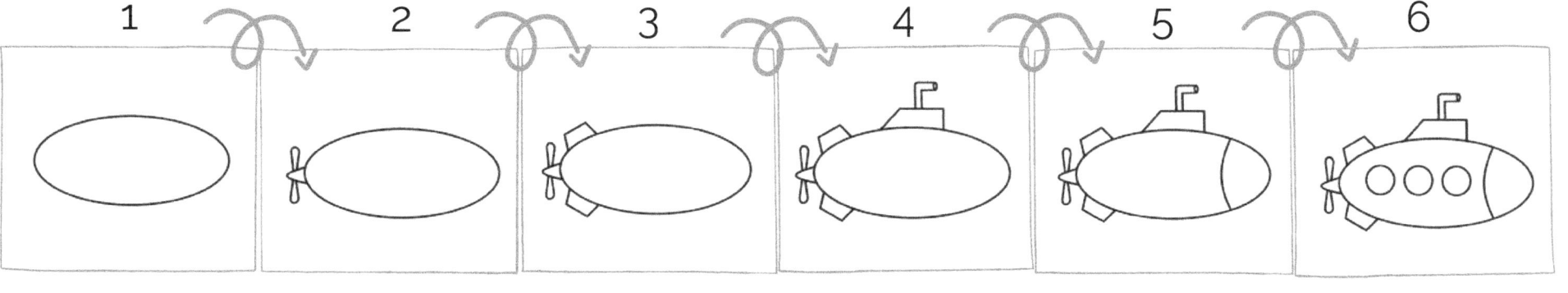

1   2   3   4   5   6

Create a Scene

Draw an ocean scenery. Add things you already know how to draw to create an awesome masterpiece. Decorate and color.

Draw each of the steps in order. Then, add details. Color to complete the picture.

Draw Here:

Owl

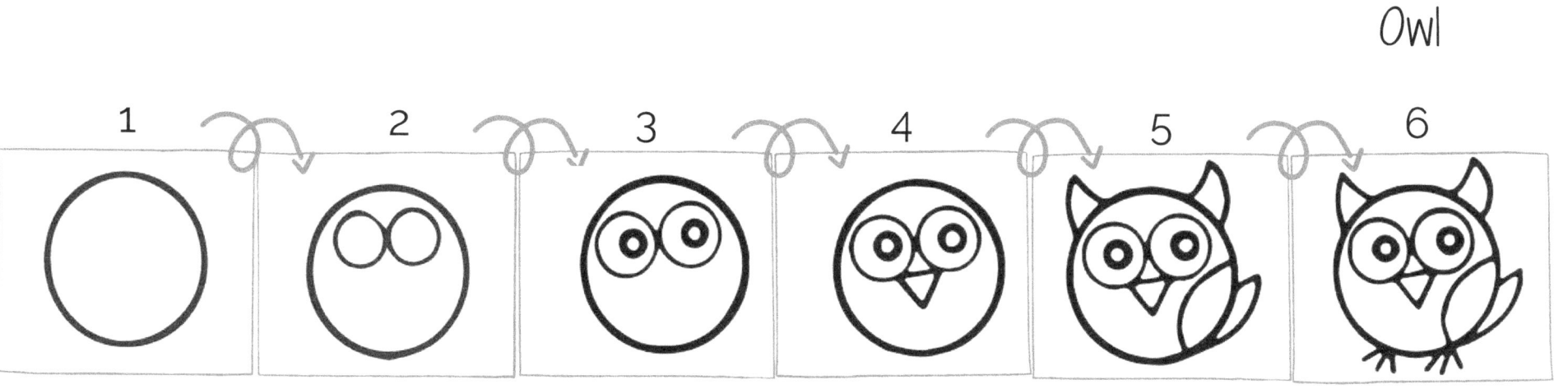

1   2   3   4   5   6

Draw each of the steps in order. Then, add details. Color to complete the picture.

Draw Here:

Owl on a branch

1   2   3   4   5   6

Draw each of the steps in order. Then, add details. Color to complete the picture.

Draw Here:

Chicken

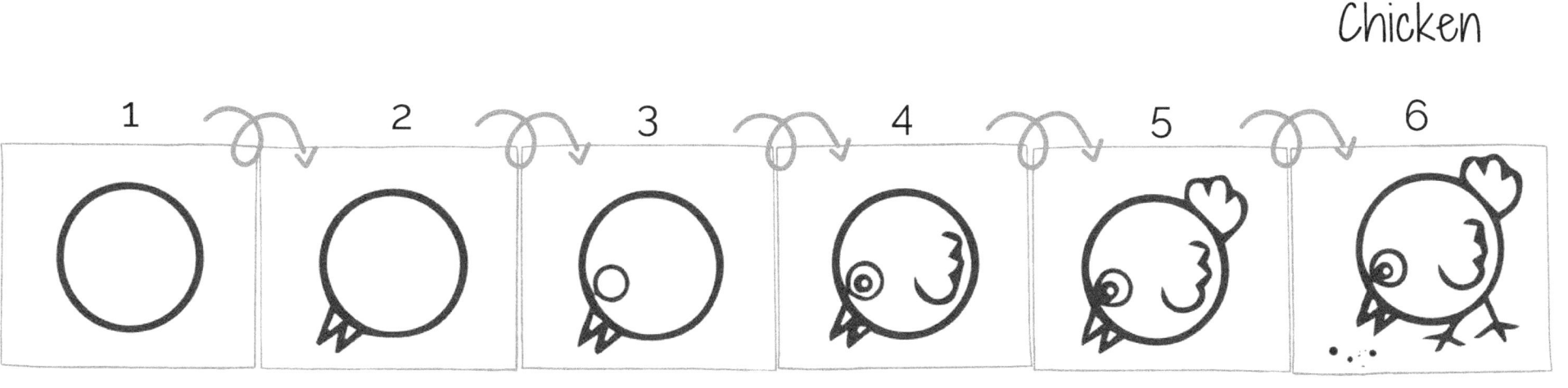

1   2   3   4   5   6

Draw each of the steps in order. Then, add details. Color to complete the picture.

Draw Here:

Hen

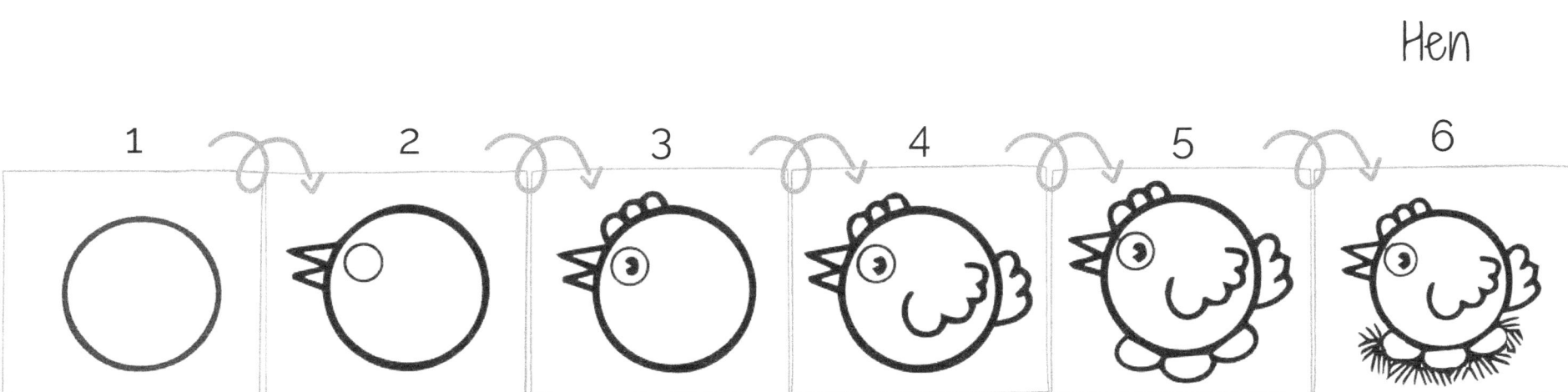

1   2   3   4   5   6

Draw each of the steps in order. Then, add details. Color to complete the picture.

Draw Here:

Rooster

1   2   3   4   5   6

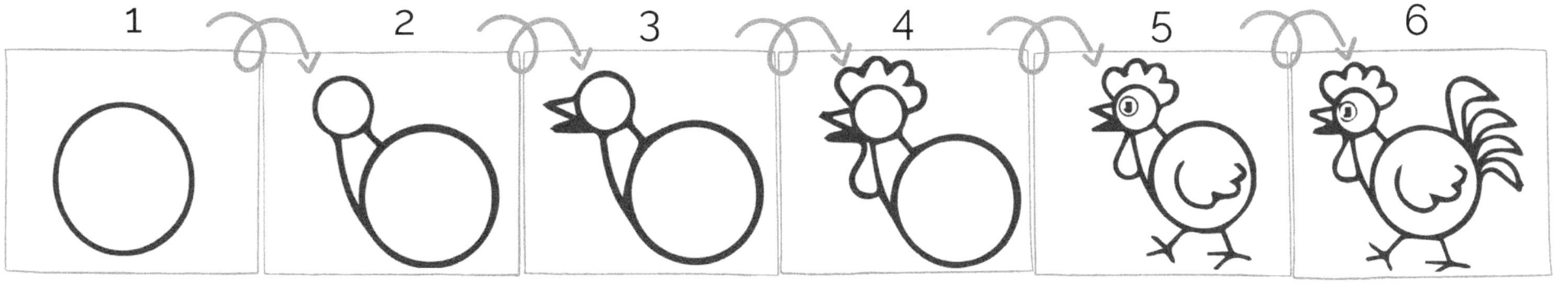

Draw each of the steps in order. Then, add details. Color to complete the picture.

Draw Here:

Turkey

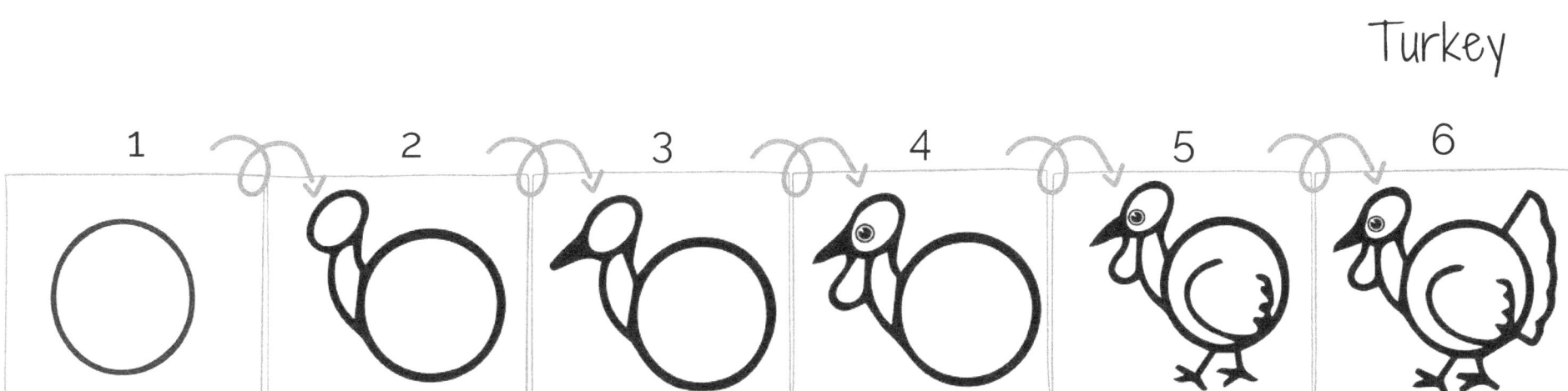

1 2 3 4 5 6

Draw each of the steps in order. Then, add details. Color to complete the picture.

Draw Here:

Eagle

1   2   3   4   5   6

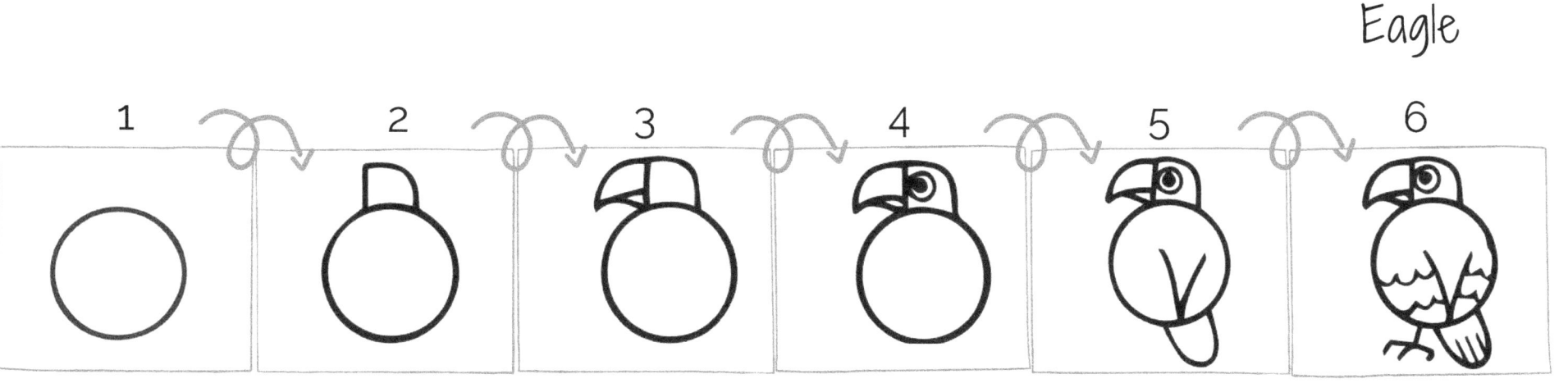

Draw each of the steps in order. Then, add details. Color to complete the picture.

Draw Here:

Bird

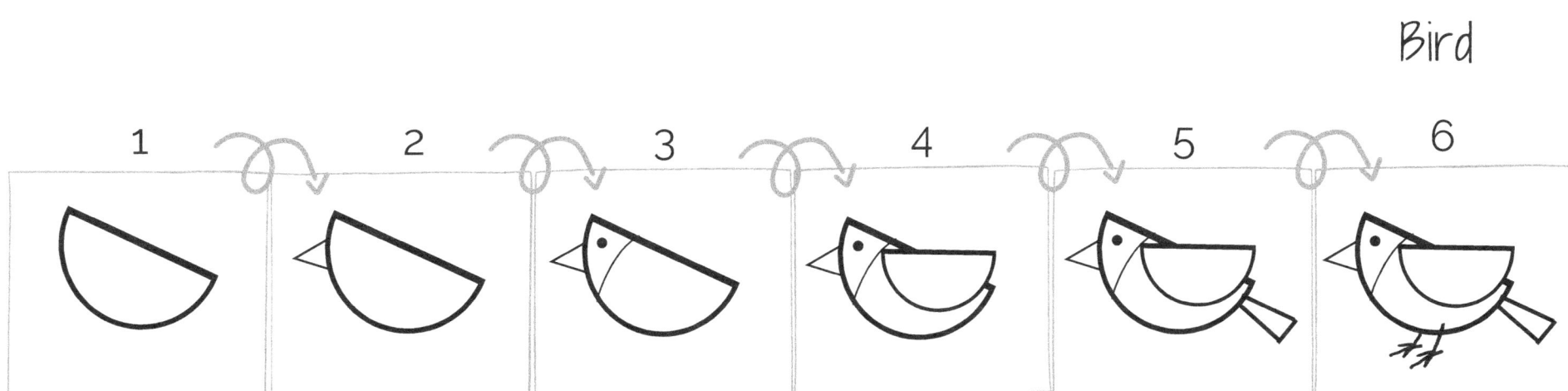

1   2   3   4   5   6

Draw each of the steps in order. Then, add details. Color to complete the picture.

Draw Here:

Birdcage

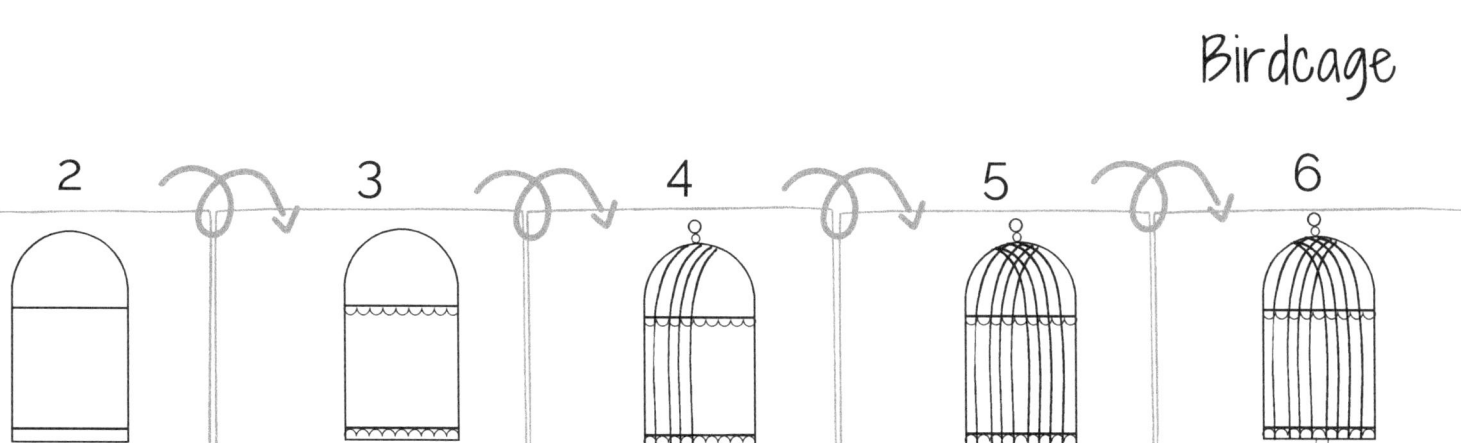

1   2   3   4   5   6

Create a Scene

Draw a bird in a cage. Add things you already know how to draw to create an awesome masterpiece. Decorate and color.

Draw each of the steps in order. Then, add details. Color to complete the picture.

Draw Here:

Cow

1   2   3   4   5   6

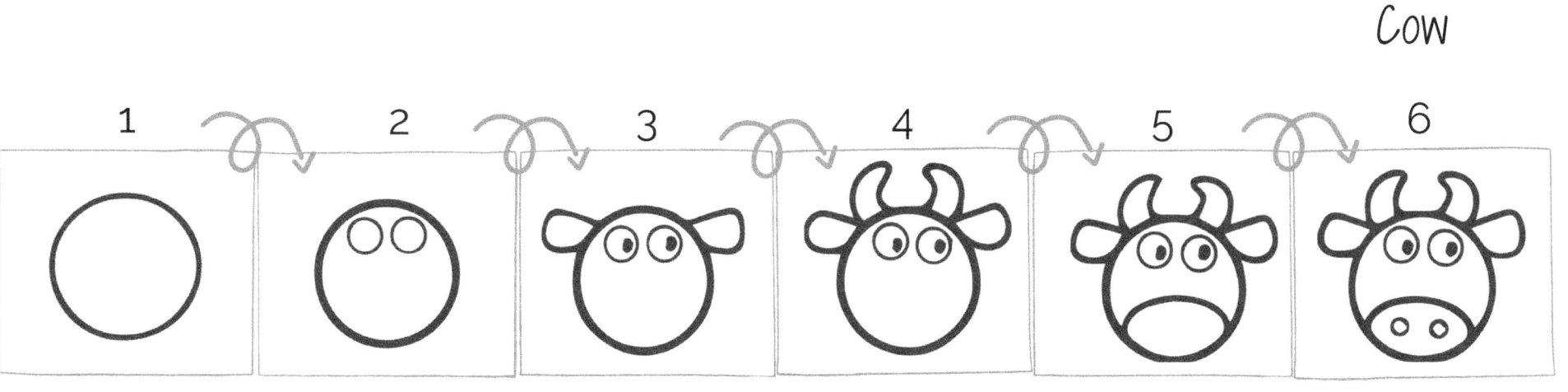

Draw each of the steps in order. Then, add details. Color to complete the picture.

Draw Here:

Milk Cow

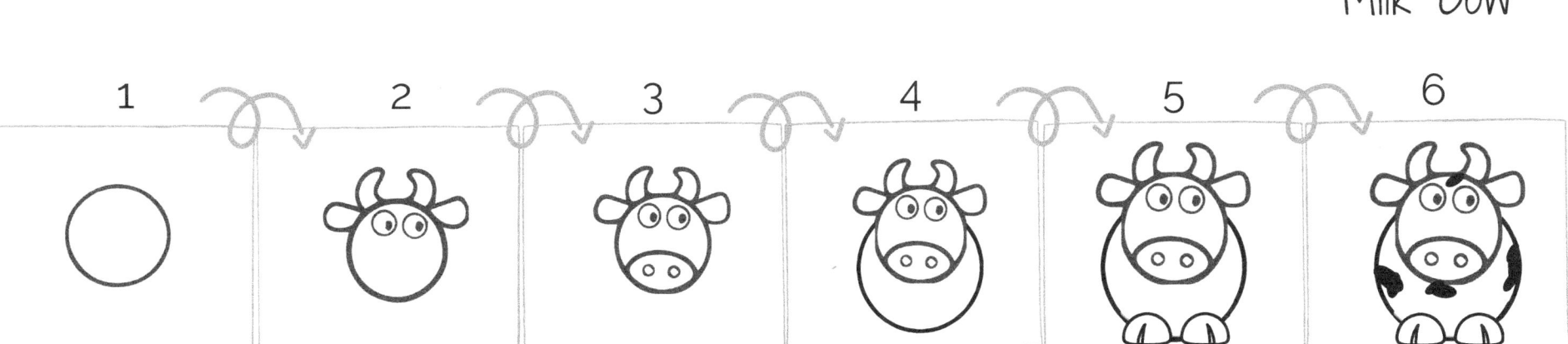

1   2   3   4   5   6

Draw each of the steps in order. Then, add details. Color to complete the picture.

Draw Here:

Bull Head

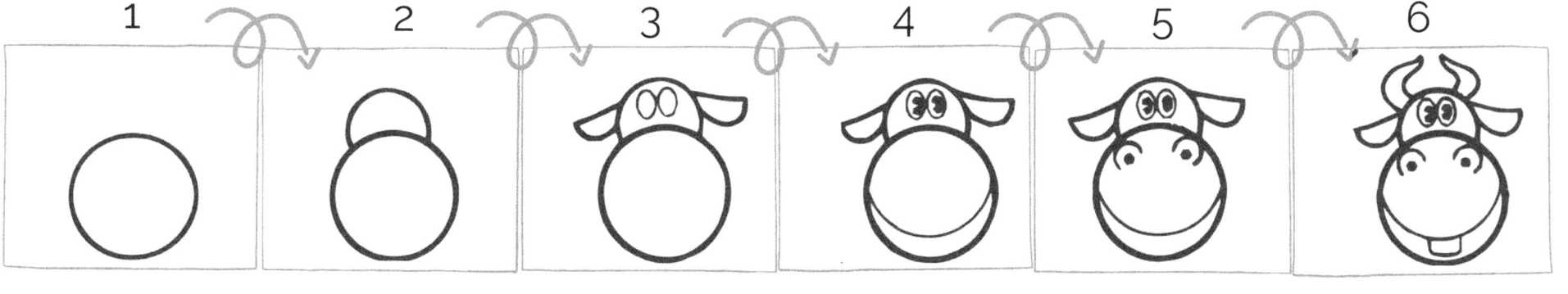

1   2   3   4   5   6

Draw each of the steps in order. Then, add details. Color to complete the picture.

Draw Here:

Bull

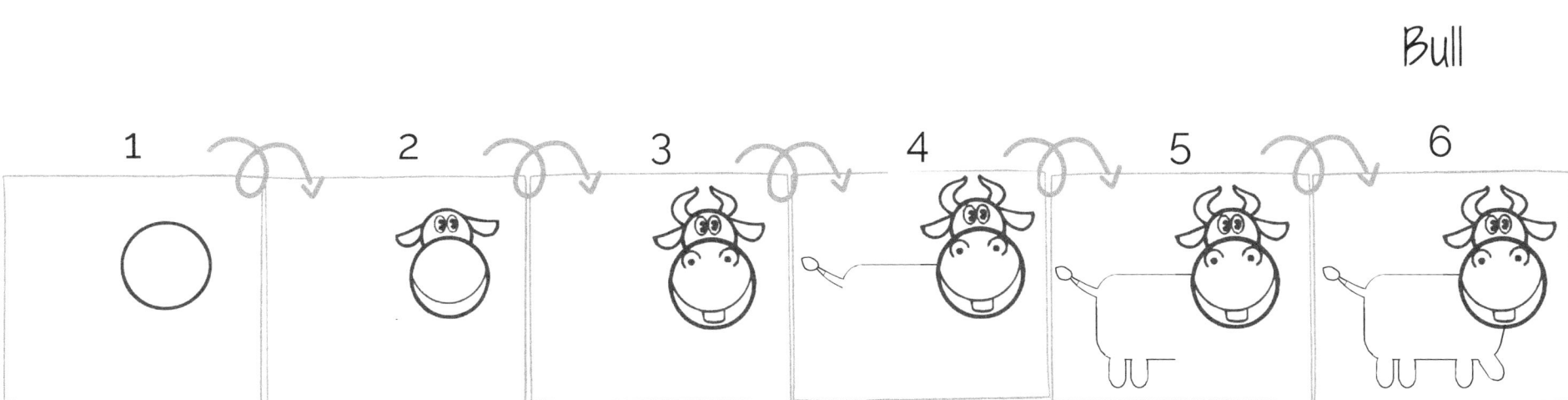

1   2   3   4   5   6

Draw each of the steps in order. Then, add details. Color to complete the picture.

Draw Here:

Windmill

1   2   3   4   5   6

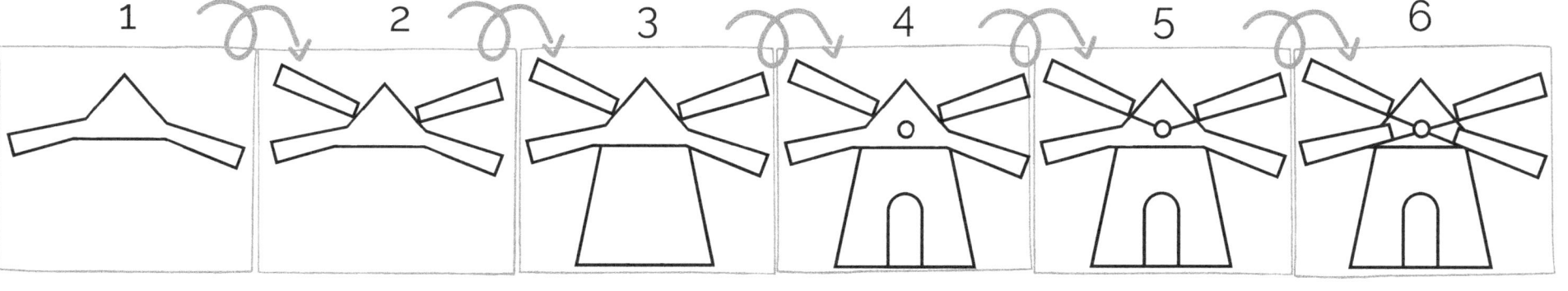

Draw each of the steps in order. Then, add details. Color to complete the picture.

Draw Here:

House

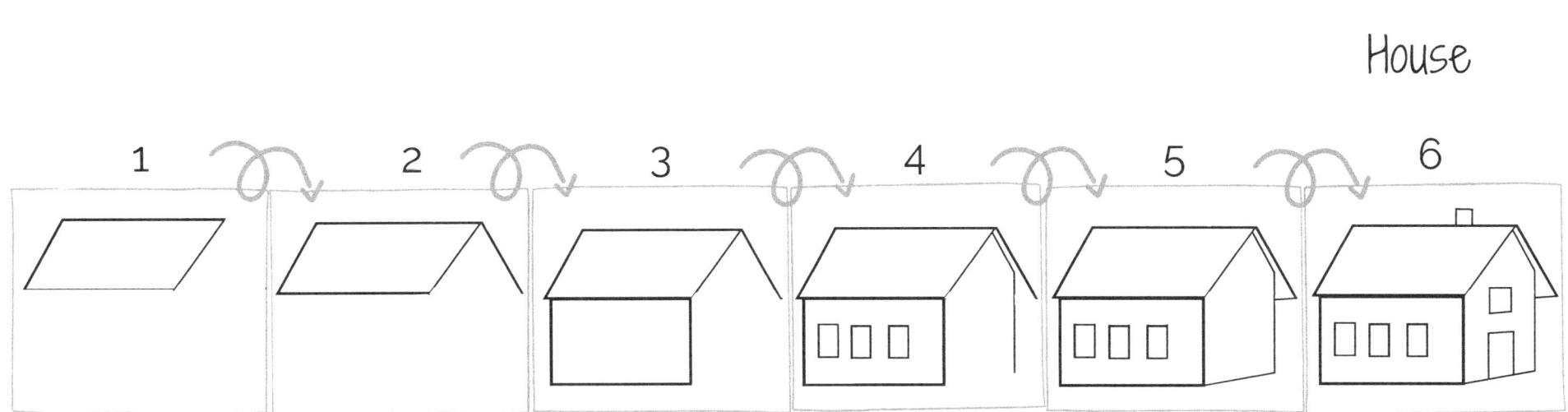

1 2 3 4 5 6

Draw each of the steps in order. Then, add details. Color to complete the picture.

Draw Here:

Truck

1   2   3   4   5   6

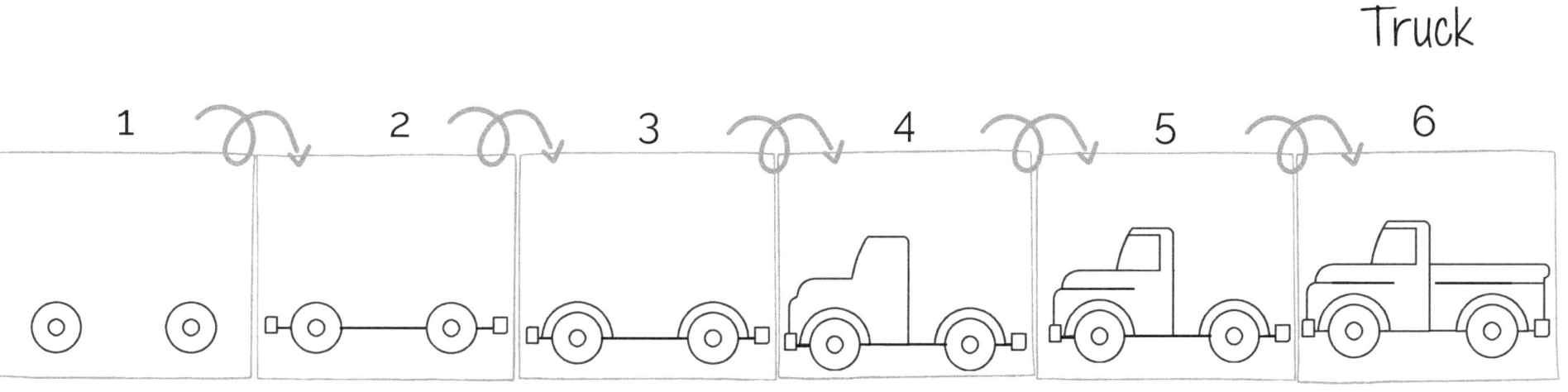

Draw each of the steps in order. Then, add details. Color to complete the picture.

Draw Here:

Tractor

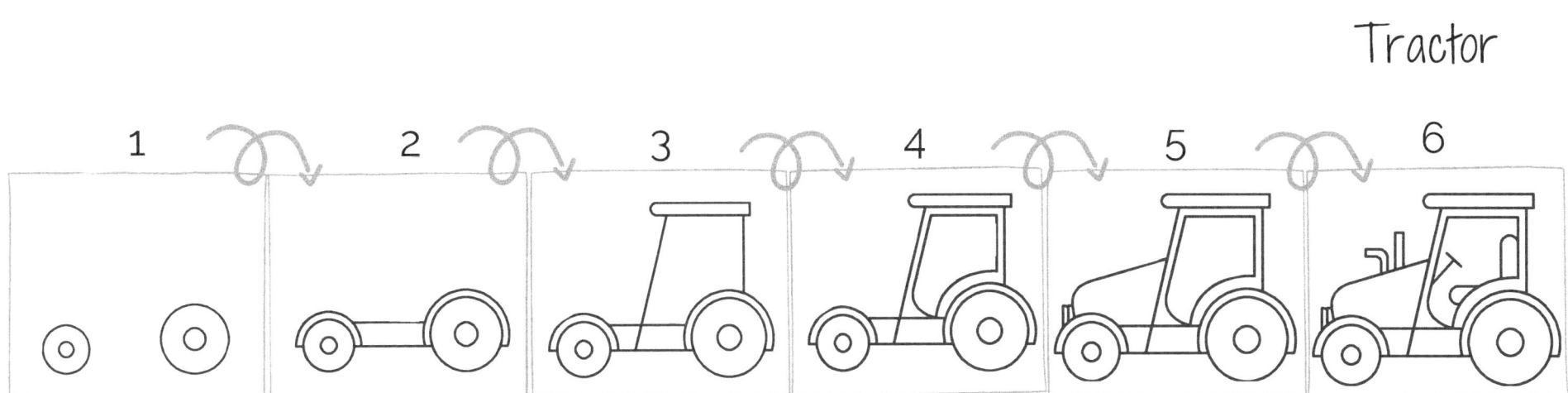

1   2   3   4   5   6

Draw each of the steps in order. Then, add details. Color to complete the picture.

Draw Here:

Scene

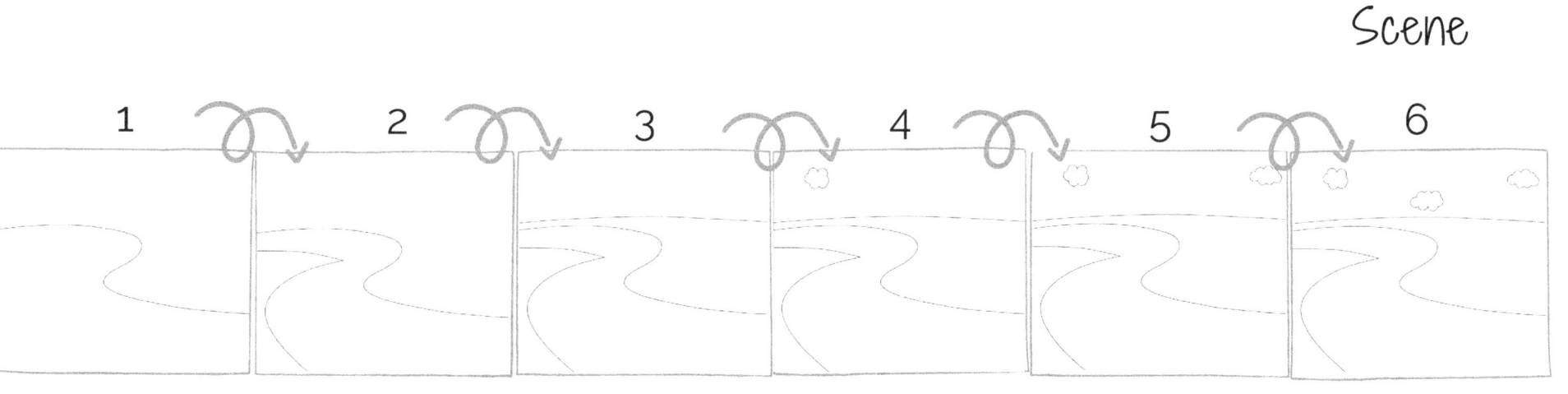

1   2   3   4   5   6

Create a Scene

Draw a scene with a truck on a road. Add things you already know how to draw to create an awesome masterpiece. Decorate and color.

Draw each of the steps in order. Then, add details. Color to complete the picture.

Draw Here:

Sun

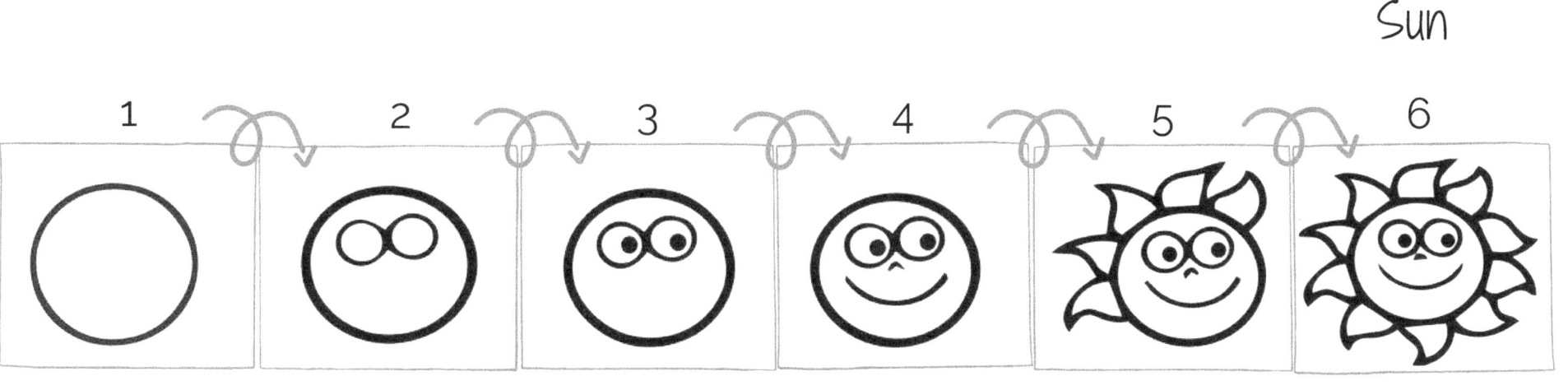

1   2   3   4   5   6

Draw each of the steps in order. Then, add details. Color to complete the picture.

Draw Here:

Barn

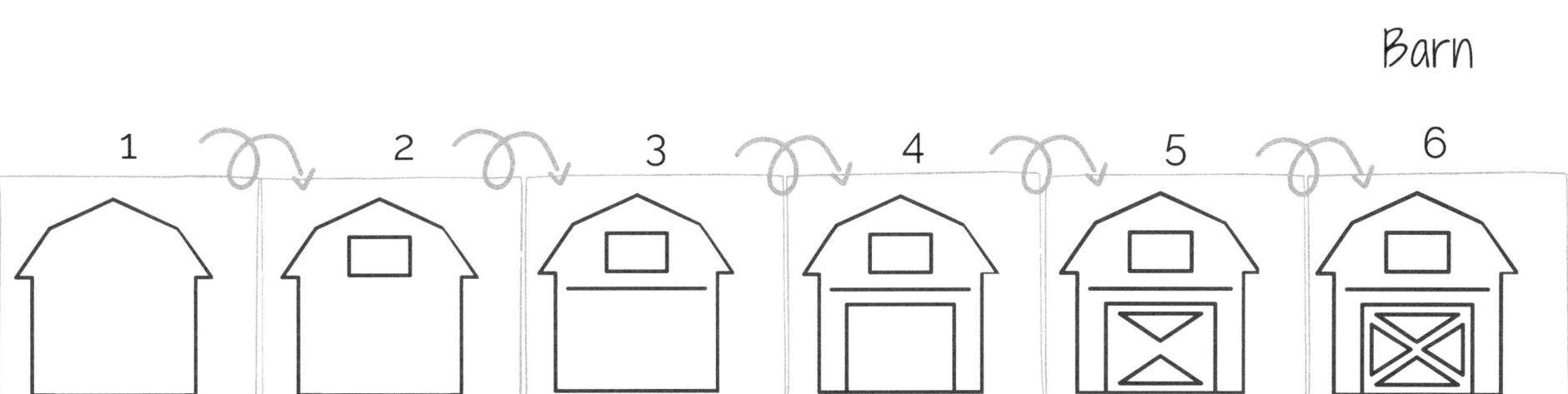

1 2 3 4 5 6

Draw each of the steps in order. Then, add details. Color to complete the picture.

Draw Here:

Pig

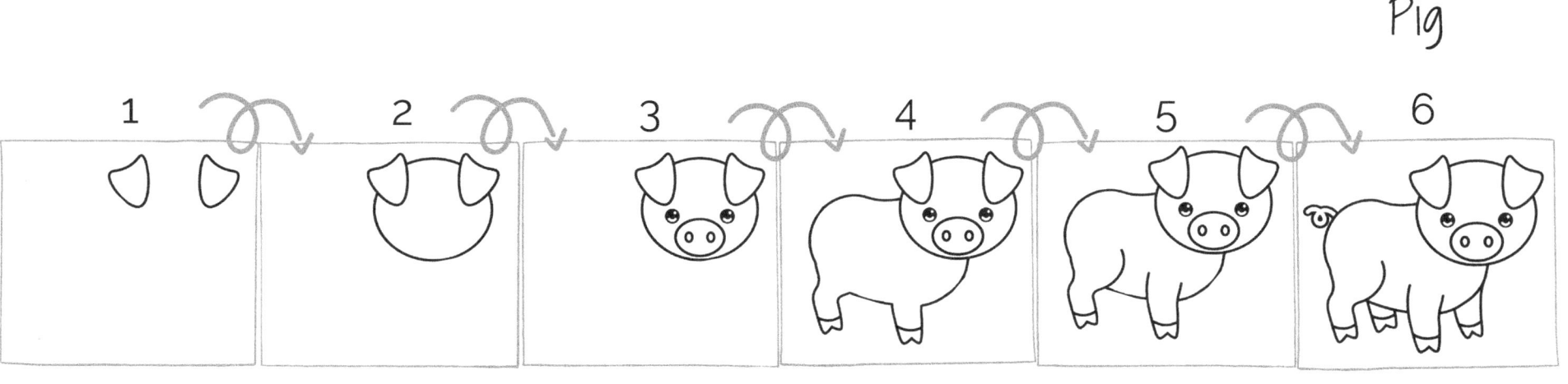

Draw each of the steps in order. Then, add details. Color to complete the picture.

Draw Here:

Horse

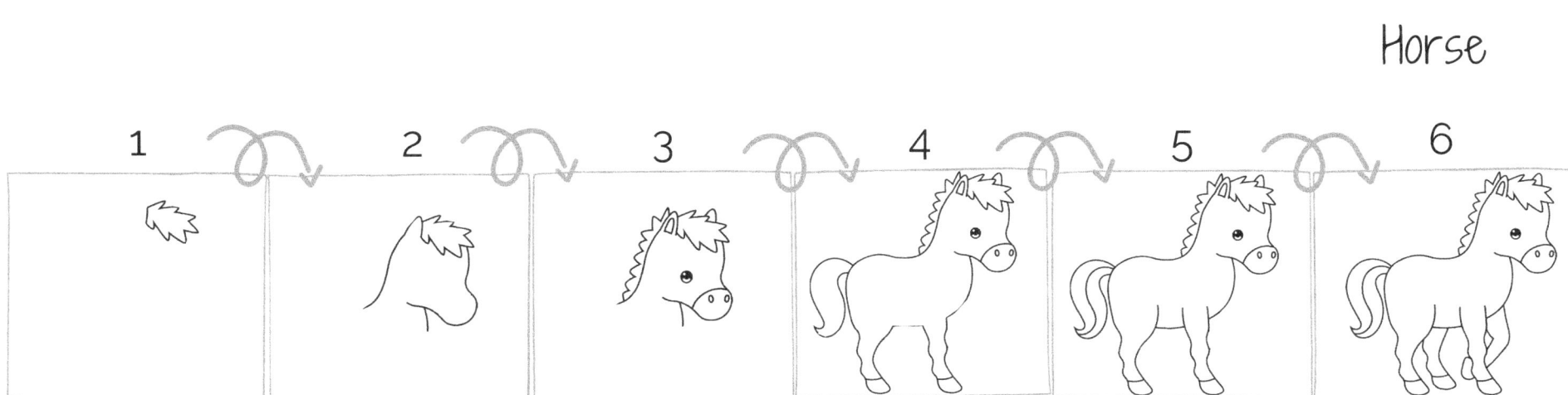

1   2   3   4   5   6

Draw each of the steps in order. Then, add details. Color to complete the picture.

Draw Here:

Sheep

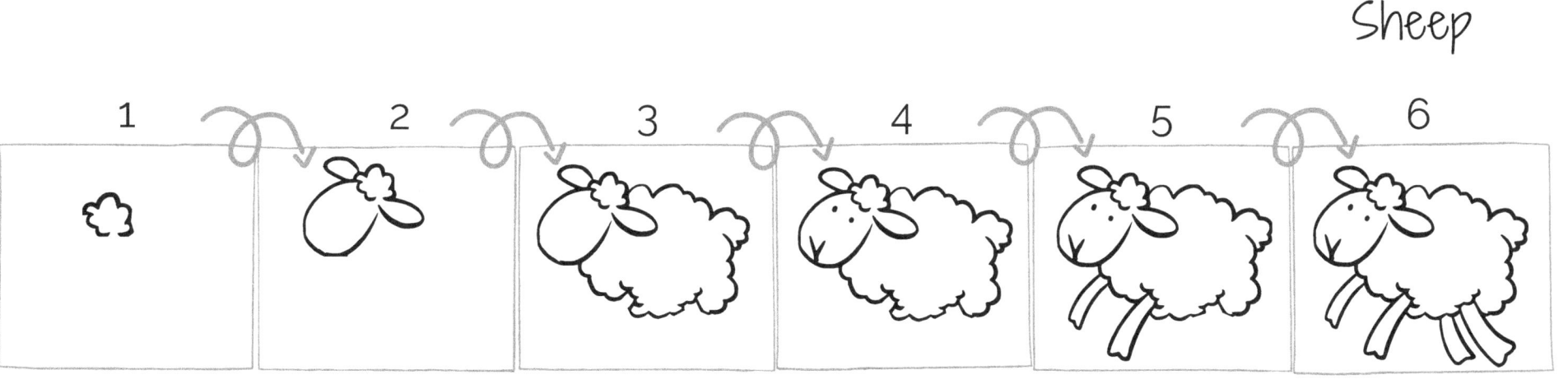

1 2 3 4 5 6

Draw each of the steps in order. Then, add details. Color to complete the picture.

Draw Here:

Apple

Orange

1   2   3   4   5   6

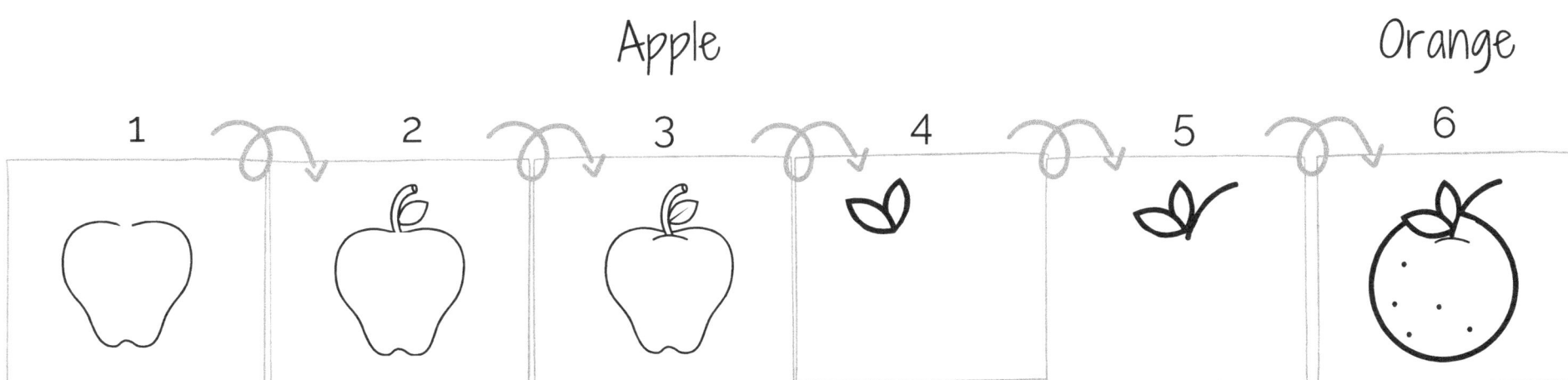

Draw each of the steps in order. Then, add details. Color to complete the picture.

Draw Here:

Tree

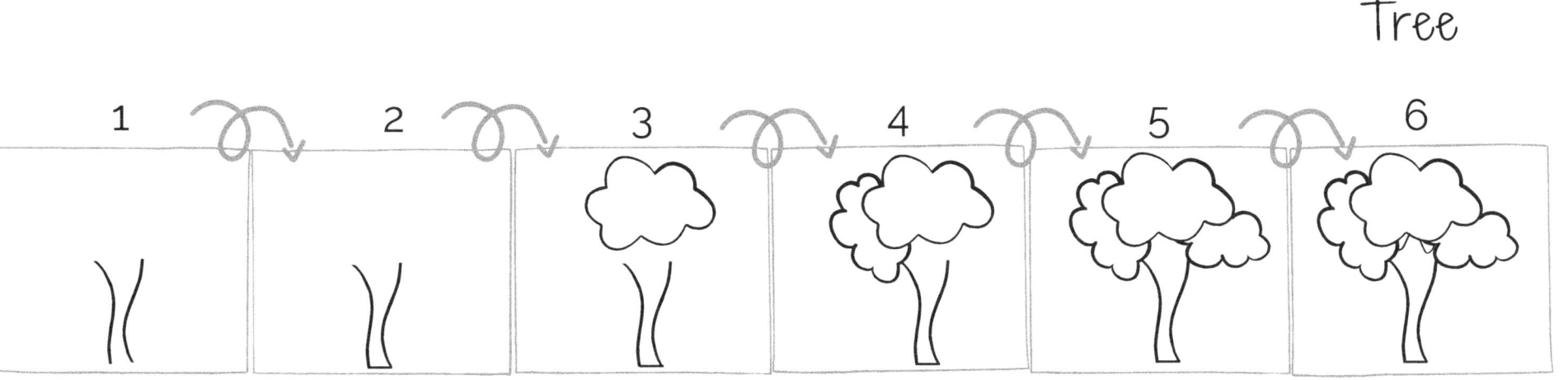

1   2   3   4   5   6

Draw each of the steps in order. Then, add details. Color to complete the picture.

Draw Here:

Tree

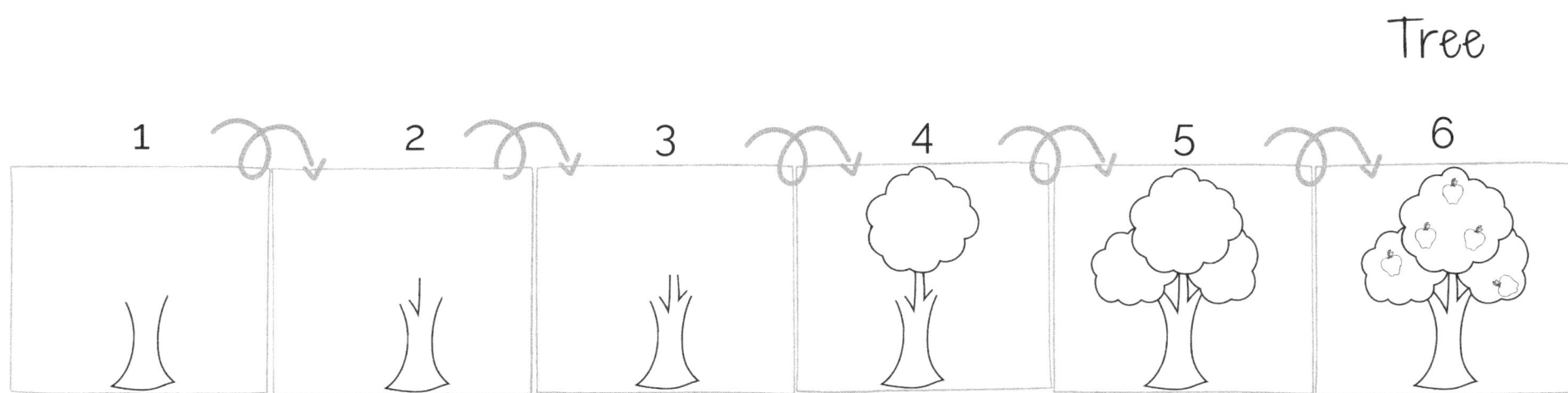

1   2   3   4   5   6

Draw each of the steps in order. Then, add details. Color to complete the picture.

Draw Here:

Sunflower

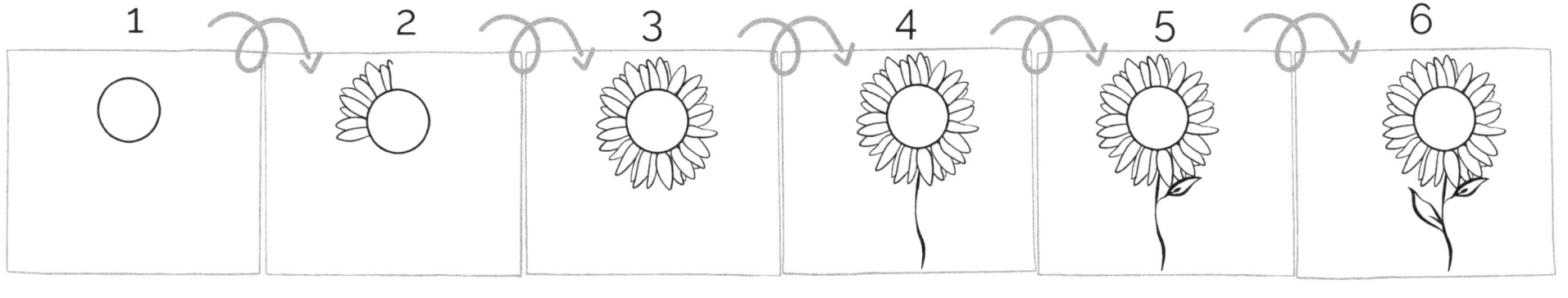

1   2   3   4   5   6

Draw each of the steps in order. Then, add details. Color to complete the picture.

Draw Here:

Ladybug

1   2   3   4   5   6

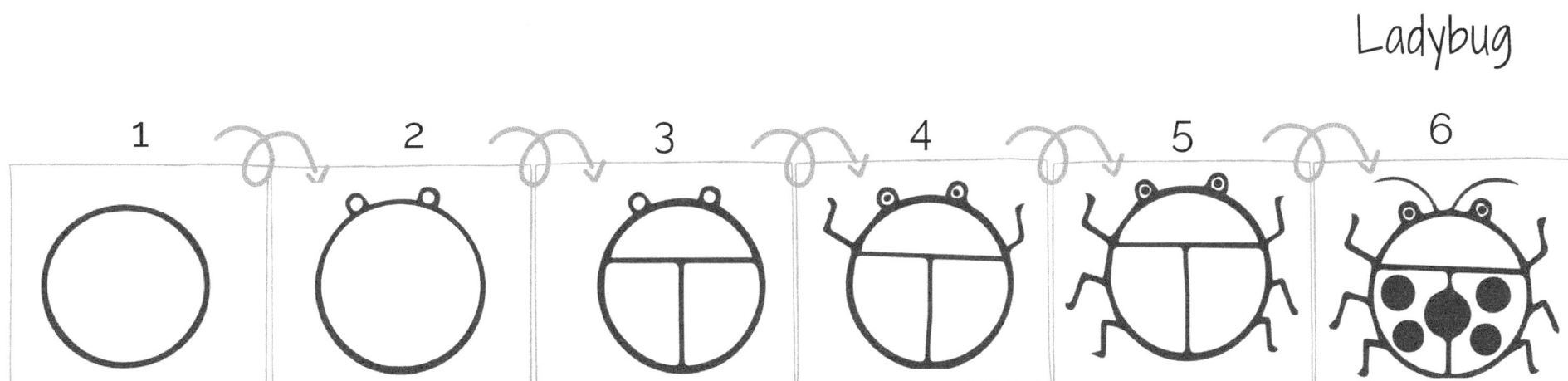

Draw each of the steps in order. Then, add details. Color to complete the picture.

Draw Here:

shovel

1   2   3   4   5   6

Draw each of the steps in order. Then, add details. Color to complete the picture.

Draw Here:

rake

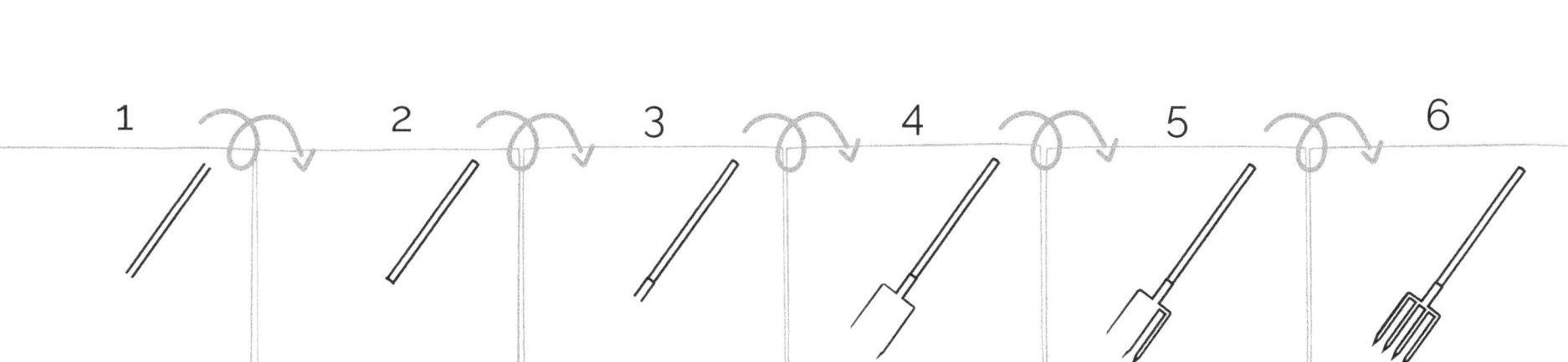

Draw each of the steps in order. Then, add details. Color to complete the picture.

Draw Here:

Girl's face

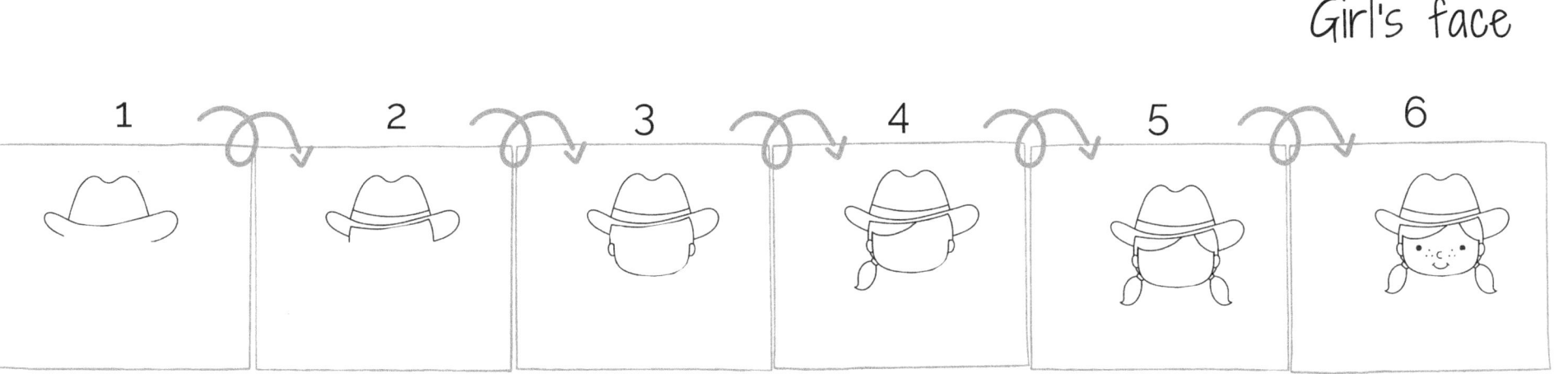

1 2 3 4 5 6

Draw each of the steps in order. Then, add details. Color to complete the picture.

Draw Here:

Farmer (girl)

1   2   3   4   5   6

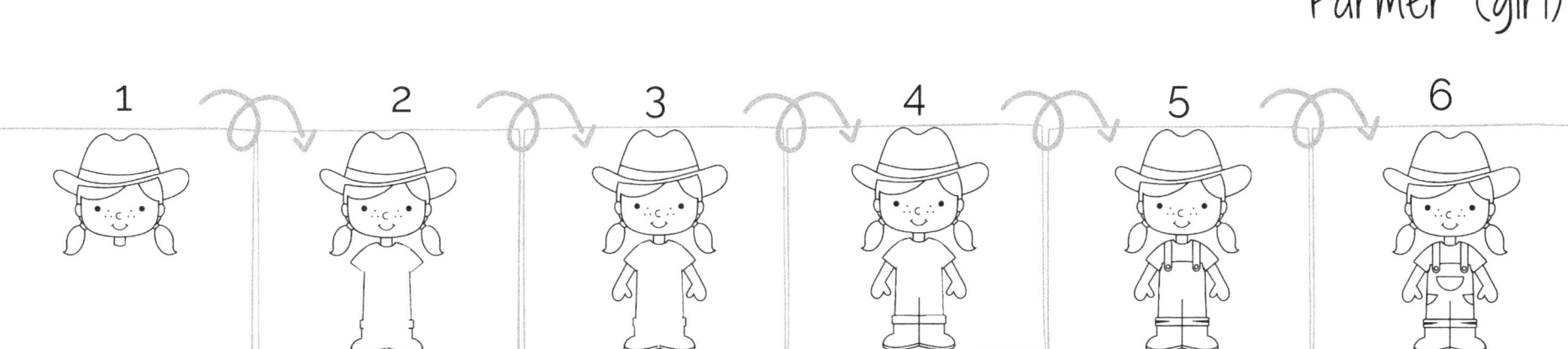

Draw each of the steps in order. Then, add details. Color to complete the picture.

Draw Here:

Boy's face

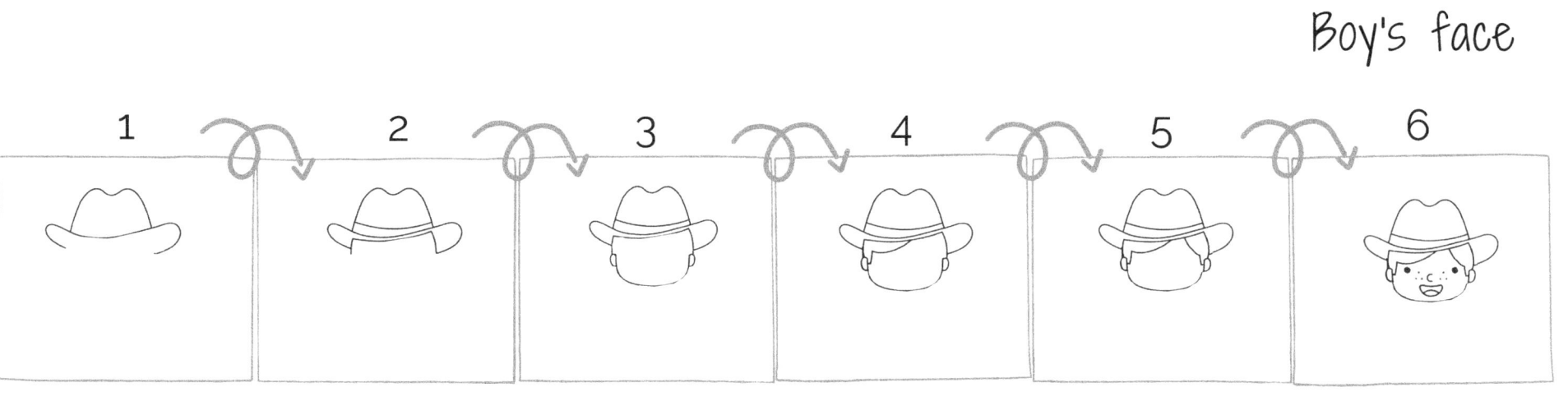

Draw each of the steps in order. Then, add details. Color to complete the picture.

Draw Here:

Farmer (boy)

1   2   3   4   5   6

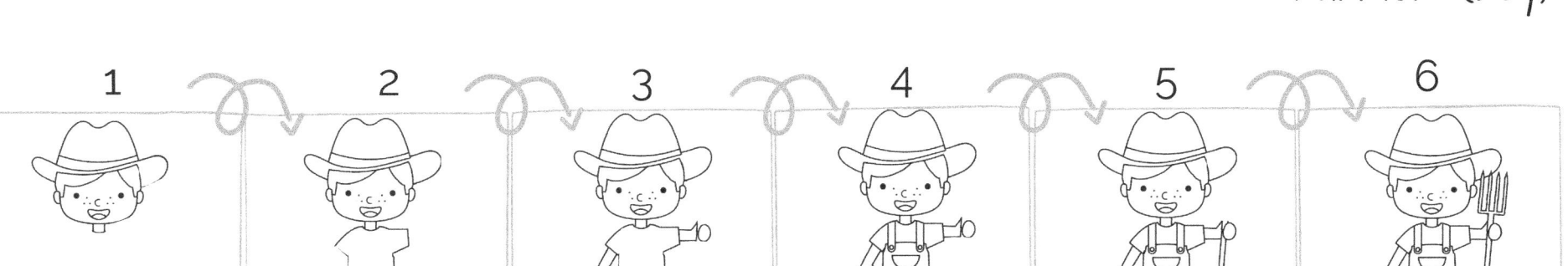

Draw each of the steps in order. Then, add details. Color to complete the picture.

Draw Here:

Boy

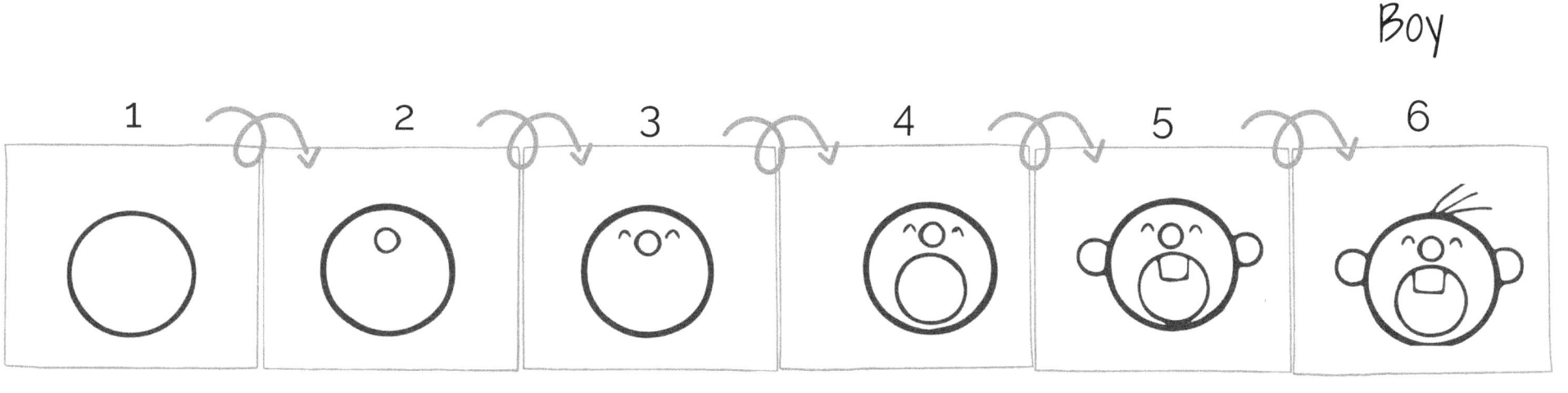

1 2 3 4 5 6

Create a Scene

Draw a farm. Add things you already know how to draw to create an awesome masterpiece. Decorate and color.

Draw each of the steps in order. Then, add details. Color to complete the picture.

Draw Here:

Monkey

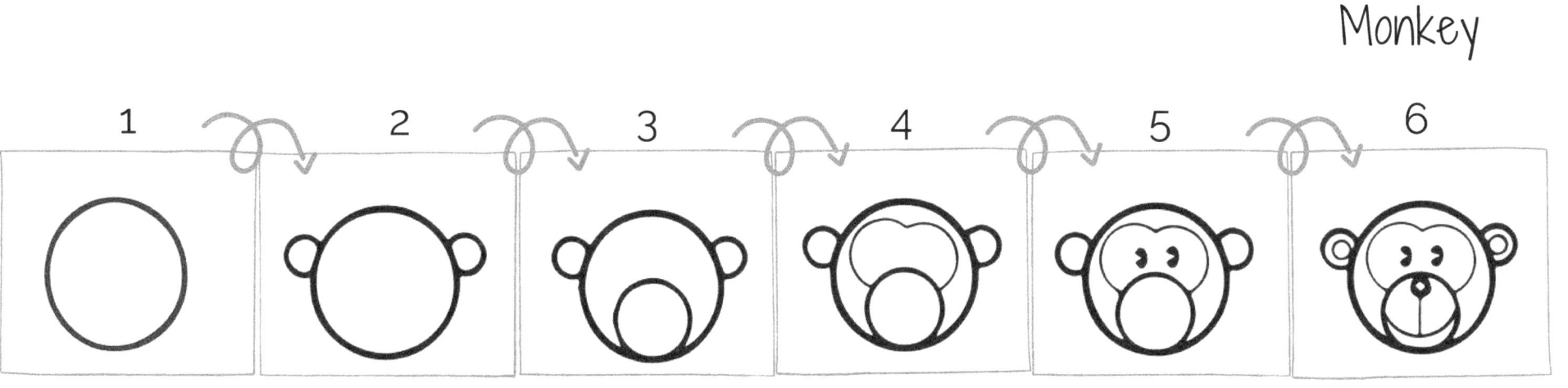

1   2   3   4   5   6

Draw each of the steps in order. Then, add details. Color to complete the picture.

Draw Here:

Mouse

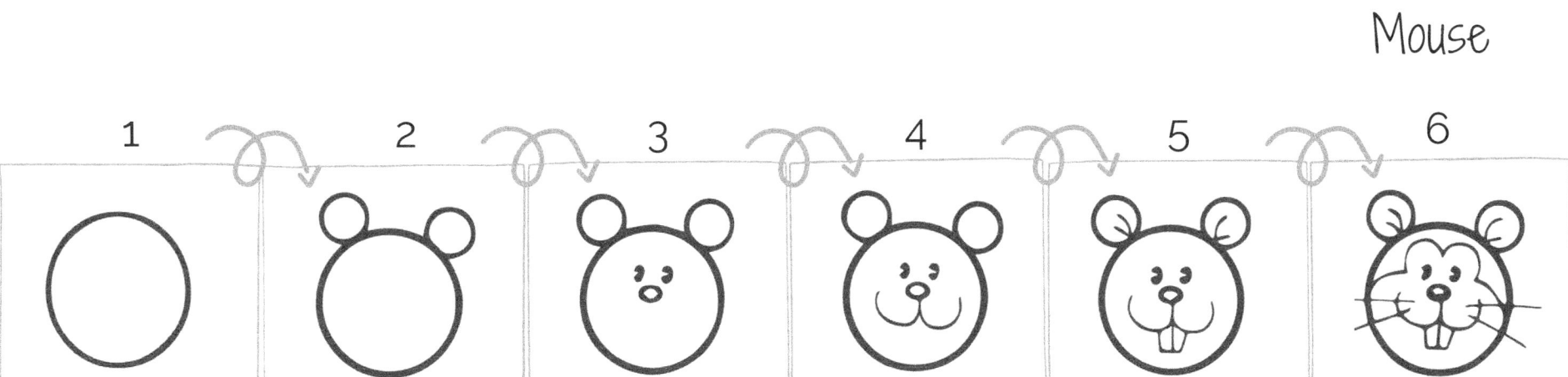

1   2   3   4   5   6

Draw each of the steps in order. Then, add details. Color to complete the picture.

Draw Here:

Dog

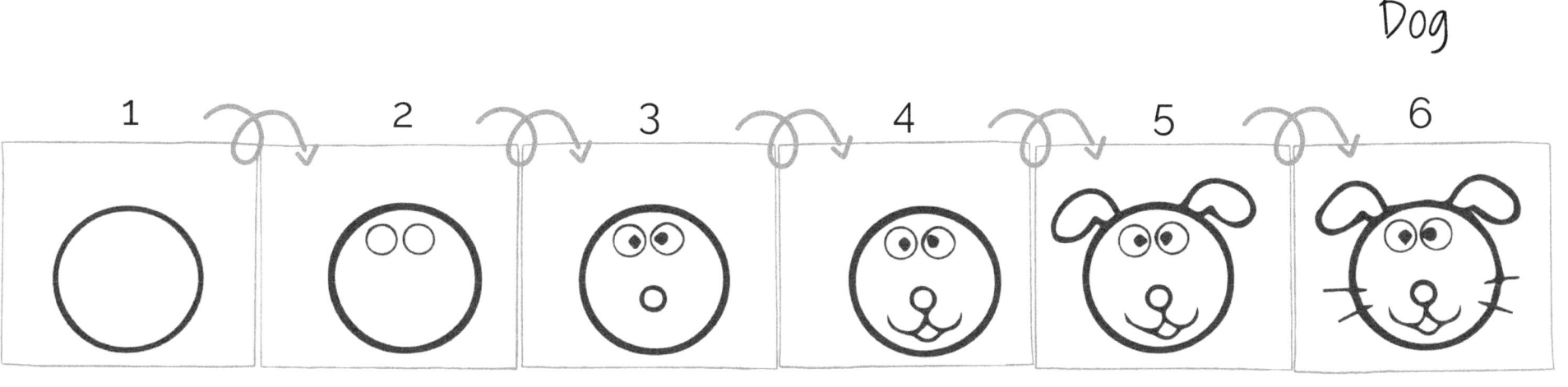

1 2 3 4 5 6

Draw each of the steps in order. Then, add details. Color to complete the picture.

Draw Here:

Cat

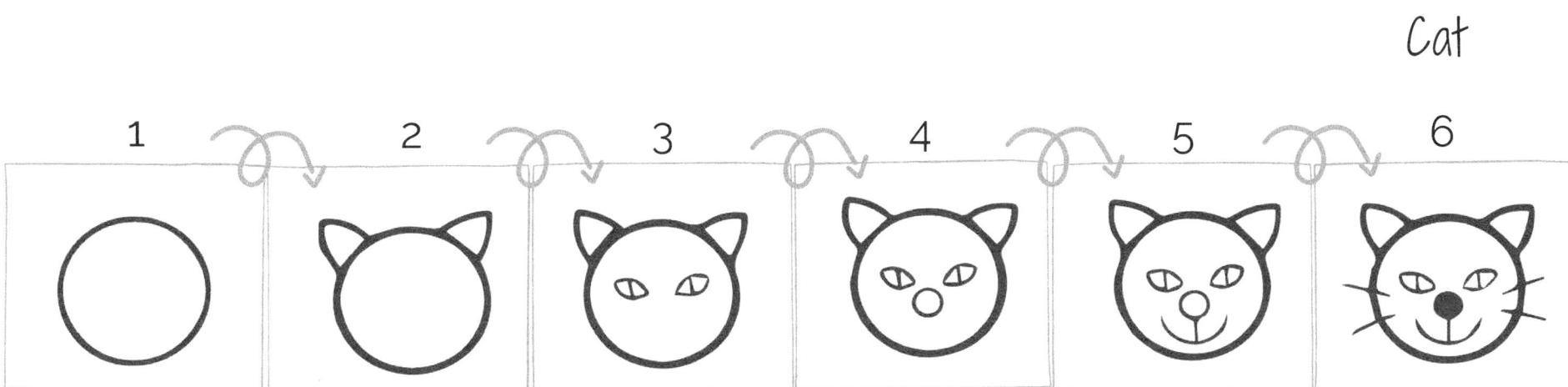

1   2   3   4   5   6

Draw each of the steps in order. Then, add details. Color to complete the picture.

Draw Here:

Bear

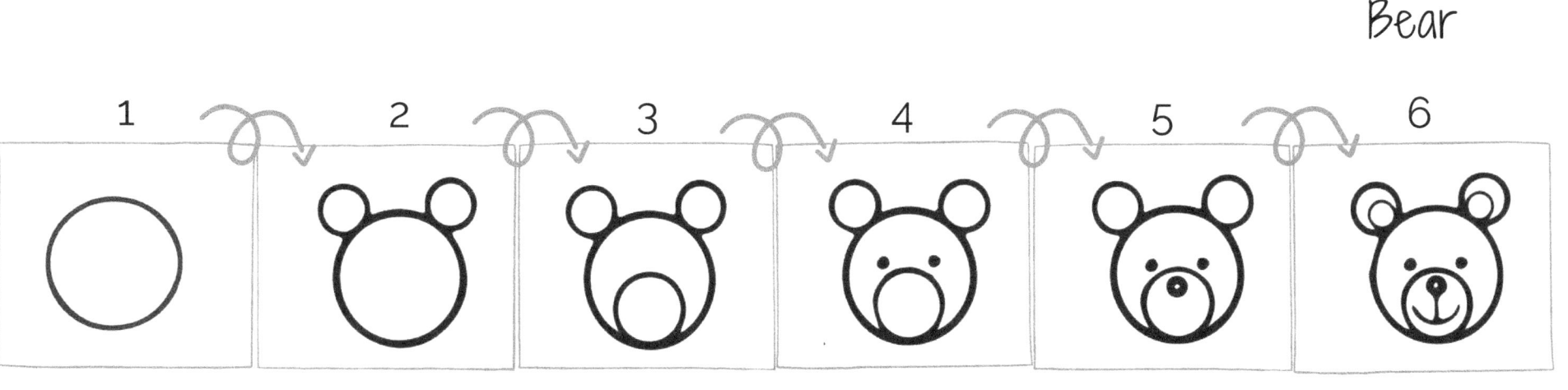

1   2   3   4   5   6

Draw each of the steps in order. Then, add details. Color to complete the picture.

Draw Here:

Panda

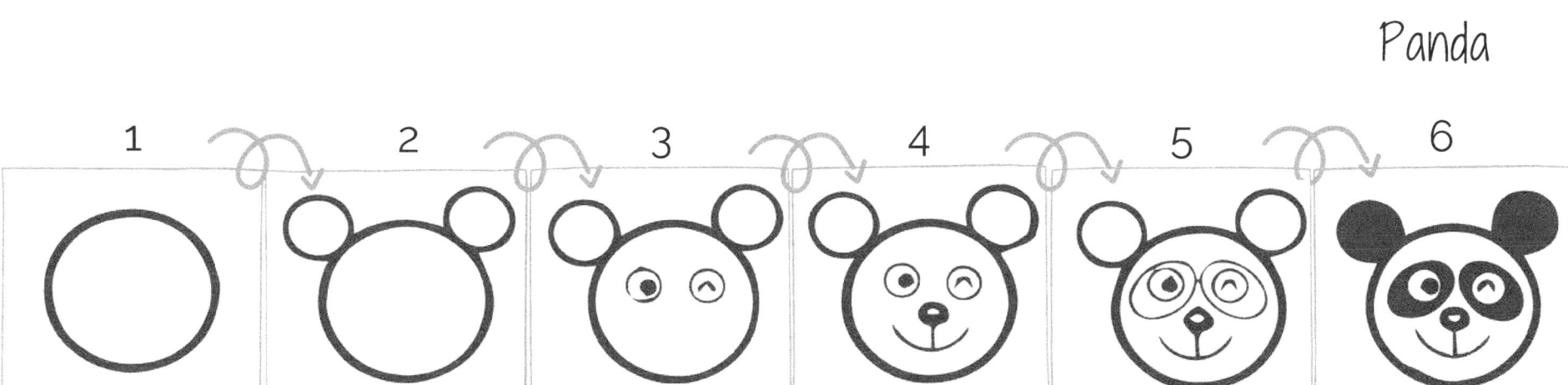

1 2 3 4 5 6

Draw each of the steps in order. Then, add details. Color to complete the picture.

Draw Here:

Rabbit

1 2 3 4 5 6

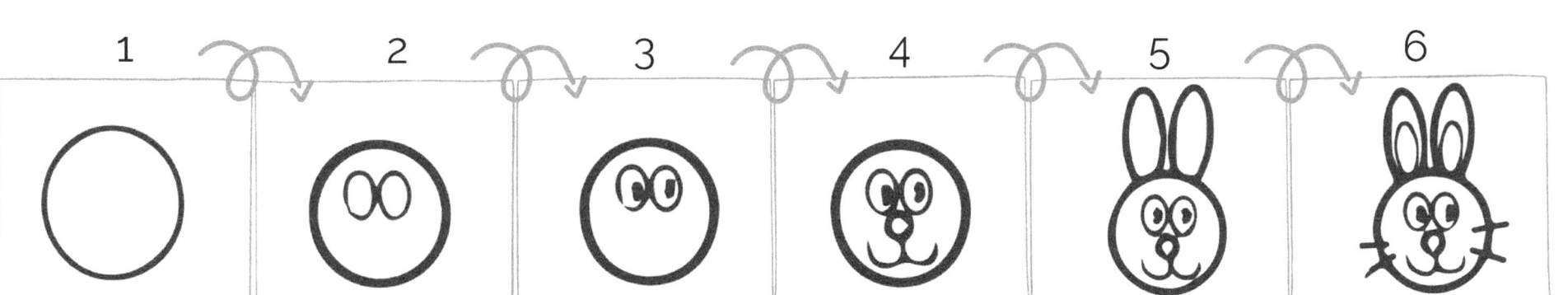

Draw each of the steps in order. Then, add details. Color to complete the picture.

Draw Here:

Rabbit

1   2   3   4   5   6

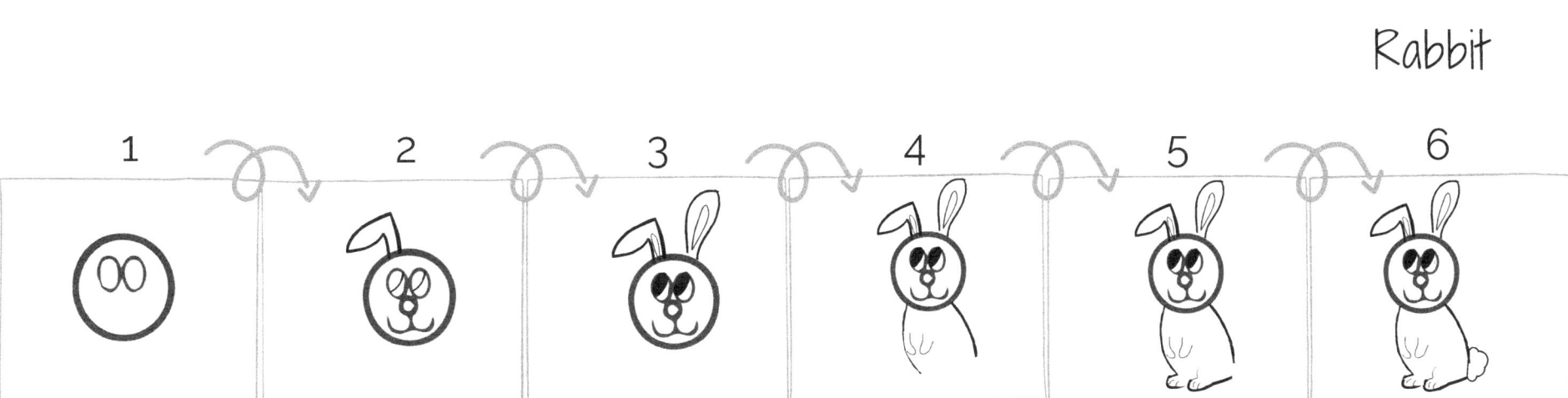

Draw each of the steps in order. Then, add details. Color to complete the picture.

Draw Here:

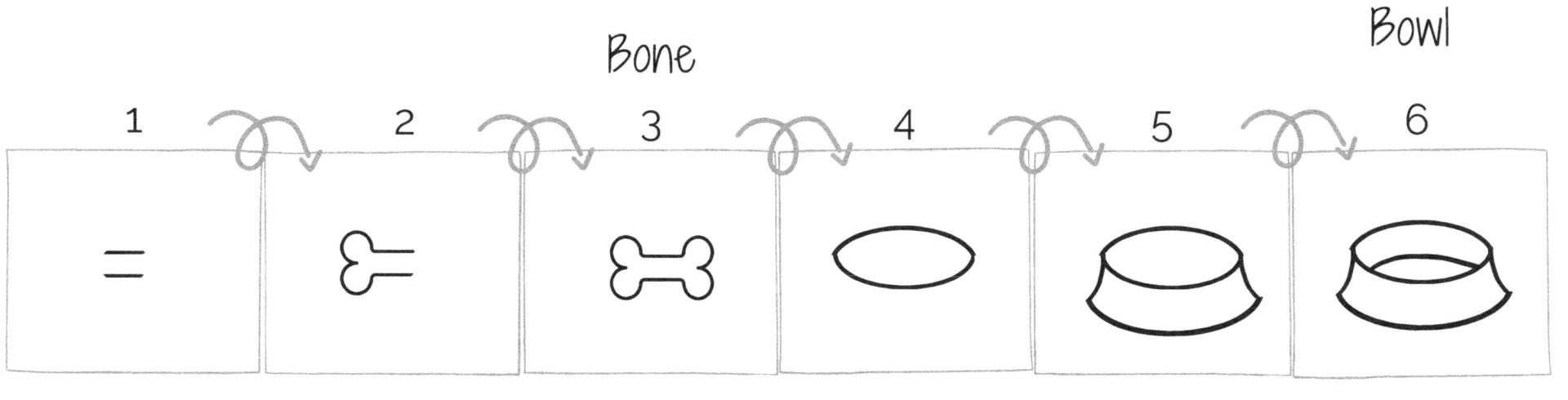

Bone

Bowl

1   2   3   4   5   6

Draw each of the steps in order. Then, add details. Color to complete the picture.

Draw Here:

Fish in a bowl

1   2   3   4   5   6

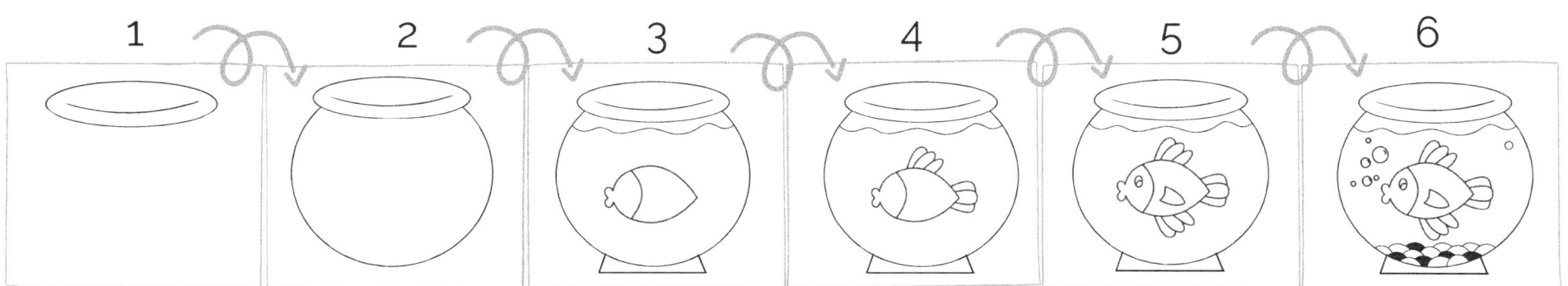

Draw each of the steps in order. Then, add details. Color to complete the picture.

Draw Here:

Clown

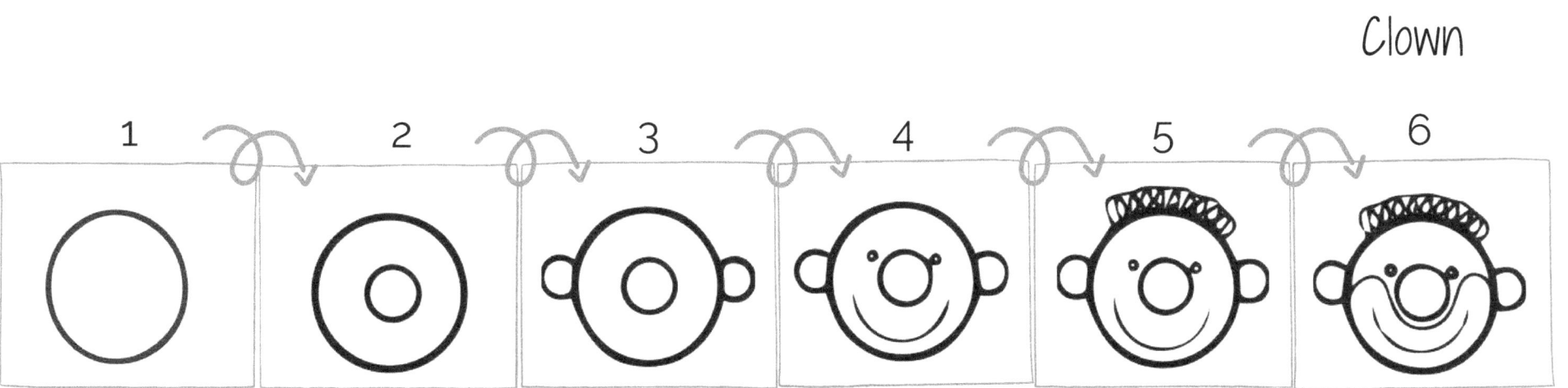

Draw each of the steps in order. Then, add details. Color to complete the picture.

Draw Here:

Soldier

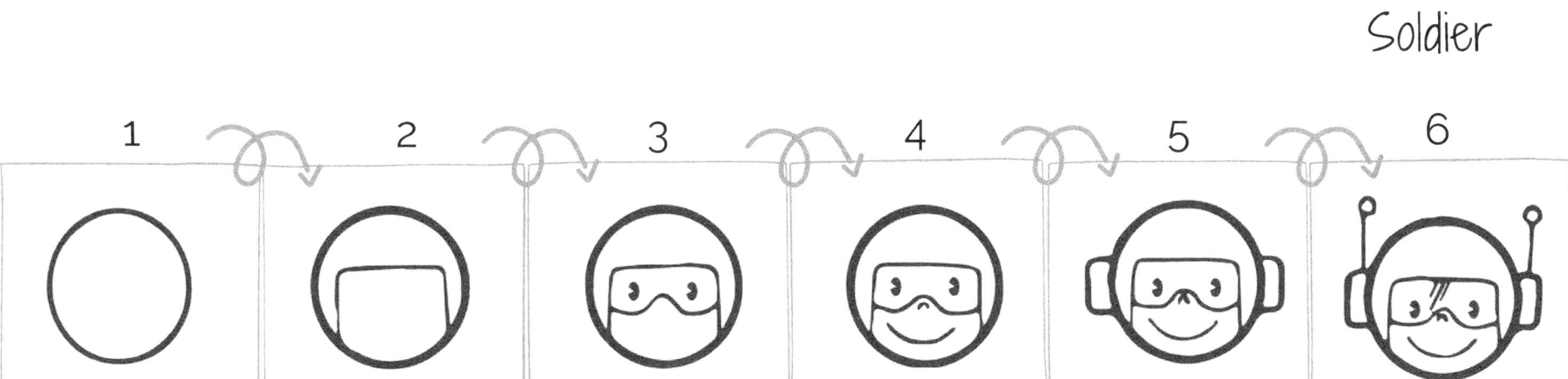

1 2 3 4 5 6

Create a Scene

Draw your own scenic masterpiece using this and the next page. Use both pages to create one big scene or two separate scenes. Decorate and color.